The Relational Revolution

Other books by Bruce Larson

The One and Only You
Ask Me to Dance
No Longer Strangers
Thirty Days to a New You
Living on the Growing Edge
Setting Men Free
Dare to Live Now
The Edge of Adventure (with Keith Miller)
Living the Adventure (with Keith Miller)
The Emerging Church (with Ralph Osborne)

The Relational Revolution

AN INVITATION TO DISCOVER
AN EXCITING FUTURE
FOR OUR LIFE TOGETHER

Bruce Larson

WORD BOOKS, PUBLISHER
WACO, TEXAS

THE RELATIONAL REVOLUTION: AN INVITATION
TO DISCOVER AN EXCITING FUTURE FOR OUR LIFE
TOGETHER
Copyright © 1976
by Word, Incorporated,
Waco, Texas 76703

Quotations from the Revised Standard Version of the
Bible (RSV), copyrighted 1946, 1952, © 1971, 1973
by the Division of Christian Education of the National Council
of the Churches of Christ in the U.S.A., and used
by permission; from the Today's English Version of the New
Testament (TEV), copyright © American Bible Society, 1966, by
permission; and from The New English Bible (NEB), © The
Delegates of the Oxford University Press and The Syndics of
The Cambridge University Press, 1961, 1970, reprinted by
permission.

ISBN 0–87680–374–5
Library of Congress catalog card number: 76–19524
Printed in the United States of America

This book is
dedicated
to the restless ones
who have
the gift of hope

CONTENTS

ACKNOWLEDGMENTS

This book exists in its present form because of the generous help and encouragement of these people:

Hazel, my wife, who collaborated from the start;

Floyd Thatcher, my editor, who helped give wings to many of the words and ideas;

Keith Miller, my friend, a leader in the relational revolution, who read the manuscript and made invaluable suggestions.

The
Relational
Revolution

Man has reached a point, occurring in our time, when an epochal change is being experienced. This change is of such magnitude and significance that it may well be judged to be of major import in the course of human evolution. At this time Man seems to be seeking tolerable levels quantitatively and is being called upon to develop qualitatively satisfying ways and means for living with himself and with others that fit what might be thought of as the scheme of Nature. . . . The choices which Man makes from the alternatives available to him will profoundly influence his own evolutionary destiny.

Jonas Salk, M.D.

I see the central meaning [of the Second American Revolution] to be a desire to achieve a person-centered society, instead of one built around materialism and large impersonal institutions which breed conformity rather than individuality and creativity.

John D. Rockefeller III
in *The Second American Revolution*

FOREWORD

SINCE I first began to speak publicly about relational theology in the spring of 1970, a growing number of clergy, laymen, and theological students have written to me expressing their interest in relational theology and asking for further help, resources, and information. And so for some time I have been gathering notes and making observations that might be of help to others who are exploring this new approach in our time.

But I found that it was impossible to write a book about relational theology without including the context in which it is taking place, for relational theology is a part of a whole relational revolution. The end product is a relational society that is affecting almost all of our present-day institutions: education, medicine, psychiatry, penology, government, and social work, as well as the institution of the church. In all these person-serving institutions, we are beginning to see a rediscovery of the worth and importance of the individual as over against content, methods, programs, techniques, theories of personality, or "the group."

In three of the books that I have written since 1970—*No Longer Strangers, Ask Me To Dance,* and *The One and Only*

You—I have tried to deal with some of the dimensions of relational theology. In this book I have attempted to deal with some of the doctrinal dimensions of relational theology in one long chapter. But most of the book is about the setting in which relational theology is growing—the setting of the whole revolution taking place in our society today.

In the next decade it is my hope that a great many other people will write on the subject, including some academically oriented people who will do a thorough job of systematizing this fresh biblical approach to theology. I already know of a number of Ph.D. candidates who are using relational theology as a basis for their dissertations. But more than writers, we need those who will explore and expand and experiment with the implications and applications of relational theology in life as it is constantly changing around us.

In this book it is my hope that the notes and the observations made will be of some help to those partners and pioneers who will discover, explore, and ultimately organize the relational revolution into which our society is already plunged and which, I believe, may ultimately be the shaping force and the blueprint for our life together.

Bruce Larson

1. PERSONHOOD—
THE KEY TO PROFITS

ON SAFARI in Africa, a wealthy American businessman got hopelessly lost in the jungle. He stumbled onto an abandoned native hut and managed to survive on a diet of berries and lizards. Many weeks later a searching party reached his shelter just as the man was about to collapse from hunger, disease, and exposure. When the rescuers burst into the hut, he raised himself up on one arm and called out weakly, "Who is it?"

"The Red Cross," came the answer.

"Sorry," moaned the dying man, "I gave at the office."

This commentary on today reflects the common experience of most of us. In twentieth-century America we no longer expect help or caring from any source, even the Red Cross. We are fast becoming accustomed to the impersonal and unfeeling services with which we are assaulted. A few personal experiences from my past week are probably similar to many you have had.

I went to the dry cleaners to pick up a suit I needed for a special occasion. Even though it had been promised for the previous day, it wasn't ready. After I had protested vigorously, the owner said, "You don't know what it's like to run a business today. Help is uncertain, customers are demanding. You ought to be glad I'm willing to clean your clothes for you."

"But," I protested, "if only you had told me there was some doubt about its being done I wouldn't have left it. I need it. I want to wear it. May I have it back?"

"I couldn't begin to find it in all this mess," he replied. "It's not ready. Nothing I can do about it."

I went to my travel agent to pick up some tickets. To my amazement I was scowled at by one of the salespeople, who muttered gruffly, "I'm busy. You'll just have to wait." After I had stood there for what seemed an unreasonable length of time, a disinterested clerk took care of me with no "thank you's" and no pleasantries. Aboard my plane later, I was met by an obviously harassed stewardess who announced, "Boy, have I had a tough day. You wouldn't believe what I've been through. I'm so pooped I'm not sure I can make it through this flight." We passengers spent the rest of the flight commiserating with the stewardess and reassuring her that everything would be all right. Obviously we didn't make any demands on her.

A day or so later I decided to enjoy the luxury of breakfast in my motel room, so I phoned room service and ordered orange juice, pancakes, and coffee. Within a few minutes the waiter arrived with a covered tray and set it on the table by the window. After accepting a handsome tip, he hurried out and I began my investigation of the tray. The pancakes looked good, but there wasn't any syrup. Impatiently, I called the dining room and complained. They promised to send the syrup up right away. Fifteen minutes later the syrup arrived, but now the pancakes were cold. "I'm sorry," I told the waiter, "but there's just no way I can eat these cold pancakes." Obviously upset, he headed back to the kitchen to get another order. After waiting another half hour, I gave up and headed out the door, already forty-five minutes late for a meeting. Who should I run into but the waiter with my second batch of pancakes. By then we were both pretty upset, so when I complained about the service, he said, "Listen, don't blame me. I'm not a professional. I'm just a student trying to make a little money. It isn't my fault if I can't get everything together here."

Now each of these episodes highlights minor annoyances, it's true, and they are not important enough to be noticed singly. Actually most of us have stopped expecting to find caring and concern from the average waiter, dry cleaner, stewardess, or ticket agent. And for the most part we have learned to struggle through without it. However, on a far more serious level, a friend tells a harrowing tale of finding the same indifference and insensitivity in a hospital situation.

First of all, she was rushed to a hospital in a strange city as an emergency patient and was made to sit in the waiting room for two-and-a-half hours while they checked her credit rating. When her friends protested, for she was too ill to do so at this point, the admitting personnel insisted they couldn't take anyone in for treatment unless payment was assured.

Finally, she was admitted and shown to a room. Later, the doctor stated he wanted some x-rays taken. So, wearing nothing but a hospital gown, this dignified middle-aged woman was pointed in the direction of the x-ray room—three floors down and two blocks away—clutching her records in one hand and trying to hold her hospital gown together in the back with the other. As she shuffled down the hall she was exposed to public gaze in every corridor and elevator.

Unfortunately, the x-rays revealed that she needed serious surgery. While she was recovering from it the most humiliating experience of all occurred. Without asking her permission and totally insensitive to her embarrassment, the teaching doctor brought a host of interns into her room, turned back the sheets, pulled up her nightgown, and began to explain her unique condition and the kind of surgery that had been performed.

Well, we can easily fault the hospitals or the medical profession for ignoring the relational needs of people. But the church and the clergy are often guilty of the same thing. Many of us head for church hoping to hear something about a God who makes sense out of no sense, a God who cares for us in spite of everything and who says I love you and forgive you. Instead, the sermon frequently has nothing to do with our need and, rather, seems to reflect the preacher's latest interest. We get a short course in biblical archaeology or we mentally traipse around the Holy Land with him. That ludicrous story about the lost man and the Red Cross applies all too often to the church as we know it. More and more churches are empty on Sunday morning because people no longer find personal help in the service. Instead they are exhorted to do more, give more, pray harder, or help someone else spiritually, politically, socially.

What does all of this say? For me it says that we are suffering on every level because of the tragic loss of the relational dimension in our daily lives. From the checkout girl at the supermarket to the doctor treating us for a desperate illness, we are being treated less and less like human beings of innate dignity and worth.

But I believe there are signs of hope. The relational revolution is on its way—a revolution in which we are discovering that people are more important than the goods sold them, the services given them, the curriculum taught them, or the sermons preached at them.

Recently, my wife, Hazel, and I flew from San Francisco to Atlanta on a Delta Airlines jumbo jet. It was Sunday afternoon and every seat was filled. We couldn't even sit together. My seat partner, another Florida resident, hadn't been home for ten days, and he just couldn't wait to see his wife and two small sons.

But, halfway across the continent, a call came over the loudspeaker for a doctor. There were two doctors on board, and they rushed to the back of the plane where a little three-month-old baby was apparently dying. They alternated in giving mouth-to-mouth resuscitation to the infant. Shortly the plane's senior pilot appeared and consulted with the doctors, and within minutes the plane dropped down for an emergency landing at the Dallas–Fort Worth Airport, an unscheduled stop that must have cost the airline many thousands of dollars. Awaiting the plane was an emergency medical team which boarded immediately and bustled off with the baby and its family.

Now this errand of mercy must have interrupted the travel plans of almost four hundred people. Most of us had missed our Atlanta connection and probably wouldn't be able to get other flights because of the lateness of the hour and the usual Sunday night congestion. But I didn't hear a single complaint. The life of a tiny three-month-old infant was at stake. Everybody's priorities were re-sorted.

Later on, at the Delta desk, we were part of a whole throng of people being rerouted and in many cases given complimentary meals and overnight hotel accommodations. When I thanked the clerk, he said, "You know, it's amazing. Nobody has complained about the delay. I guess personal and business plans are unimportant compared to one small life."

If we are to experience a relational revolution, we need to discover our true priorities in whatever field we are serving or working. In Chicago, Marshall Field became a pioneer merchandiser when he instituted a different set of priorities for his salespeople. He insisted they were not selling goods, they were serving people. His salespeople were indoctrinated with the slogan that the customer is always right. Another of Mr. Field's slogans was, "Give the lady what she wants!" Understanding that good relationships with customers was the primary goal, Marshall Field's became one of the most remarkable stores of all time.

We are no longer in an industrial age. That has slipped into the past with the agricultural age. The age ahead, I am convinced, will be service-oriented, and we must move into the relational era to survive. Money will be made primarily by providing services rather than by supplying goods or products. Understandably, in our computerized society people are tired of being treated as things or as consumers. We need to assert our humanity. To do this, we may need people to massage us, entertain us, walk our dogs, clean our homes, wax our cars, cut our grass, and a host of other services. Behind all of this is the profound desire deep in our hearts to be treated as persons and thereby find or regain our dignity.

Big business is already being confronted with this fact. There is presently a leadership crisis in industry. Younger executives trained for top positions are leaving in their middle years just as they are about to become vice-presidents or general managers. These men and women are opting out. More money or larger stock options or the key to the executive washroom is no longer incentive to stay. More and more employees want a chance to be creative, to have a louder voice in decision-making or operational procedures which communicate that they are worthwhile people who are taken seriously and treated with dignity. Without this kind of motivation, the much-needed top executives in harness are going to drop out in even greater numbers to buy a marina in Florida or open a hunting lodge in Maine.

The relational revolution is at the heart of this service-oriented era ahead and the institutions that recognize it will surely prosper and become pacesetters. But, as I said earlier, we must first come to the place where we are able to think through and discover our true priorities, both individually and in society. Our present institutions are in serious trouble today, but I believe their rebirth will herald the relational society ahead.

2. THE RELATIONAL SOCIETY

"IT WAS THE best of times; it was the worst of times." This much-quoted opening from *A Tale of Two Cities* can be said of any time. Life is bitter or sweet depending upon what you see, your perspective. For me these are exciting times—times of change, when a quiet (and not-so-quiet) revolution is taking place.

God Is Doing a New Thing

A cynical philosopher once said, "Everything that needs to be said has already been said. But since nobody was listening we'll have to say it again." How many sermons have you heard by preachers who believe that? "I told you last Sunday and the Sunday before so I'll tell you again: God loves you." The message that emerges is, "There is nothing new. God is not going to do anything new. It's all been done. We're living out pages of a play already written."

Personally, I believe that God is waiting and willing to reveal things that will radically change the lives of people. I believe that he is eternally waiting and eager to call forth something from you that has never been said or thought of by anyone else since the beginning of time. You may be the one in your own field or area of interest to find that all the good things haven't been said or done or even thought of.

Often we are hampered in our search because we want to hold on to "new" things that have become old. Some truths are timeless, like the law of gravity or the grace of God in Jesus Christ. But most of the things we call "truths" are transient—relevant and illuminating for a short time only —though they often become the vestibules for new and larger or more relevant truths.

My father was sixty when I was born. Though he was old in years (to my embarrassment, friends who came to the house usually assumed he was my grandfather), he was a radical and youthful thinker, prophesying future events that seemed unthinkable, like topless swim suits for women at a time when bathing suits had long sleeves and bloomers. He was the first person I knew of his generation to choose cremation. He said it was the wave of the future.

I will never forget the day the first radio came into our house. I want you to know that radio completely revolutionized life in the Larson household. For the first time we could be where the news was happening and hear it at that very moment. Hearing, "live," the abdication of the King of England and subsequently the coronation vows of his brother stunned and thrilled all of us with its implications. President Roosevelt became a member of each American family (a loved or hated member depending upon your politics) by way of his regular fireside chats. Each evening polarized around certain radio shows. Meals and bridge games took second place to "One Man's Family," "Myrt and Marge," and "Amos 'n Andy." Even with company over, we listened to "the regulars," so great was my father's love affair with the radio.

Dad died in 1944, but had he lived a few years longer, I

know that he would have been the first in his neighborhood to own a TV set. No sentimental loyalty to old loves would have kept him from embracing a new and better love! (After all, he remembered moving from kerosene to gaslights and then from gaslights to electricity with no ill effects!)

I yearn to move forward into the future culturally, socially, and theologically with the ease that my father did technically. But it is not always easy. Some part of me is a sentimental reactionary. Several years ago I had the privilege of hearing Karl Barth lecture in the great Gothic chapel of Princeton University. The place was packed to hear one of the most influential theologians of the twentieth century. When the great old man was finished with his lecture, I felt somehow disappointed. I came to hear a revolutionary prophet, and there was not a new thing in what he had said.

I subsequently realized that Barth was one of those rare men who bring such new and fresh truths to their age that the age must change to catch up. All of us in that chapel were living in a post-Barthian world. All of Christendom, both students and detractors of Barth, were different because of him. Oliver Wendell Holmes once described the impact of a man like Barth: "Now and then men's minds and hearts are stretched by a new idea and never shrink back to their original dimensions." Well, Barth had changed theological thought so much that in that academic setting he was a status quo figure rather than a revolutionary. But on that special evening I just felt sad because it seemed to me a revolutionary had passed from the scene. Obviously I was more in love with the revolution than with the needy world!

Something like that is happening in every dimension of life and thought, as it did a few years ago to many of us who are presently middle-aged. Having discovered, with the advent of the behavioral sciences, that we have feelings of which we need not be ashamed, we are in the process of throwing off the emotional corsets that our Victorian ancestors handed down to us so faithfully. We are finding that feelings are neither good nor bad morally, that God gave us feelings as a gift and they are to be used in living life to the full. Bottled-up feelings are dangerous and potentially destructive.

Well, for those of us over thirty-five, this is a new truth. Now, we are centering much of our Christian witness and celebration and worship on this newly discovered God-given gift of our feelings. And this is as it should be.

But before we rush in to share and promote this new truth with today's young people, let us realize that most of them have grown up "doing their thing" emotionally. To promote our new truths with the younger generation could be irrelevant and possibly harmful. New truths for them might mean the discovery of responsibility in relationships to self, others, and God—the kind of responsibility that was for the most part the birthright and burden of my generation.

I guess what I'm saying above all is that all the things we hold dear—doctrines, values, ethics and loyalties—must be reexamined from time to time if we are to be a part of God's purpose for the world in relevant ways. Ours is a particularly frightening time, it seems to me, because so much of what we considered essential and inviolate to our way of life is dissipating and disintegrating. God is doing something new, and in order to accomplish it much of the old will have to go. We are in revolution.

Examining the Old Values and Attitudes

Let's look at some of those things which may be a part of this revolution. True, they are funneled through my own experiences, my own bias and prejudice, but perhaps you can hear or see them through my eyes. I really believe, though, that some of the old values and attitudes we've been communicating are grossly misleading, if not downright myths.

The energy crisis in the United States threatened some powerful changes. Our children were amazed that the first thing suggested by the "experts" was a temporary closing of the schools. Now, the bars didn't close; stores didn't close. Only the schools were affected. What does this say to our children about priorities?

The futurologists tell us we're at the end of the industrial age. We're coming into a new age, postagrarian and post-industrial. The big law, and the big lie, of the industrial age was that bigger is better. Anything good must be made bigger and better and in greater quantity. It's taken a long time to arrive at the place where we can say, "Who says bigger is better?" Now, this whole assumption is under attack. The jumbo jet has proven unprofitable, and the enormous American car is increasingly impractical and unsalable. Multimillion circulation magazines such as *Life* and *Look* have gone out of business because their very size made advertising costs prohibitive to the average company. It would appear that bigger is not always better.

Political labels which we've taken for granted for so long are becoming meaningless. While my wife, Hazel, and I were in England recently, I looked up a friend who has started an inner-city program in London's East End. The Salvation Army, the Church of England, the Congregationalists, Methodists, and all kinds of unlikely people are linked together there because they believe that Jesus wants to work in one of the great slums of our world. They are not only trying to introduce people to Christ but are burning down slum buildings as people move out and before the government can move new tenants back in. They are forcing the building of new and adequate housing as one phase of their total program. This group is trying to make a radical change in the living conditions in that area.

Interestingly, this scene of activity has traditionally been a liberal stronghold. The conservative government could never get the vote there among the working class. But the liberal representatives in that area who have been in power for years now are proving to be as resistant to change as the conservatives. These "radical" Christians are now the real liberals. And it is the old so-called liberals who are fighting the real movers for change.

Whenever a group becomes entrenched in power, it can easily lose its liberal stance. The tendency to preserve the status quo surfaces almost immediately. We in America are descendants of those pioneers who fled to the new world seeking religious freedom. But our forefathers, having attained it, were soon reluctant to offer it to other groups. (Ask Roger Williams!)

What have we learned about our contemporary values from the miserable Watergate debacle of the early 1970s? Here was a grand exposé of the treachery and hypocrisy of double standards. Those in positions of leadership seemed to say, "If I'm in power, the laws for me are different from the laws for you." It appeared that "worthy" ends legitimized nefarious means of all sorts. It is easier to preach self-control than to practice it when alone. It is easier to preach love than to be loving in specific relationships. It is easier to preach faith than really to trust God when all that matters seems to be falling apart. Perhaps Watergate is so appalling because it is so universal. I find it in me.

Nowhere have our true values been communicated in a more misleading fashion than in the area of sex. Our strange movie rating codes tell young people that nude bodies are immoral and shameful while all kinds of sadism, violence, and bloodshed are acceptable. We live in a time when it is fashionable to be sexually permissive. But here's an interesting phenomenon. An acquaintance of mine, manager of a Playboy Club, told me this strange story: "You know, the Playboy Club is the temple of the mammary gland, not of nudity. The breast is everything. But one night in this temple glorifying the breast, a young couple with their baby came in to have dinner. In the middle of the evening, the baby began to cry, and when the mother started to breast-feed the baby, the bunny girls as well as the customers were horrified and insisted that I put a stop to it." Imagine, in the temple of the mammary gland you can't use a breast to feed a baby. This is pure perversion!

It seems the old values are being examined in the psychological world as well. R. D. Laing, one of the most controversial figures in psychiatry today, is challenging both the definitions and causes of mental illness in our time. He suggests that perhaps we have so much "mental illness" in the Western world because we cannot stand suffering. As a matter of fact, we've even tried to abolish suffering. We have made every attempt to push the three great traumas of life out of sight: birth takes place in hospitals; mental patients are locked away; people die off in a corner somewhere, rather than in the bosom of their family and surrounded by friends. Laing is at least one voice saying, "What is happening in our society? Why can we not stand suffering? Suffering is a part of life."

Dr. Karl Menninger brings theological insights to the matter of mental illness in his book *Whatever Became of Sin?* when he says, "We have called sin two things. A crime, and lock people up who deviate, or we call it mental illness and

put people in mental hospitals. What about the bulk of the
problem which is neither crime nor mental illness? This is
man's willful, moral irresponsibility. Let's call it by its right
name. It's not a disease or a crime. It's sin, something deep
in the heart of man that needs changing."

Finally, let's look at our attitudes about death. From all
appearances, we in the church seem to have conspired with
the culture to play down the reality of death. Death is the
new obscenity. It is to our time what sex was to the Victorian period. When a person dies, the undertaker tries for
that "natural" look, and we send cards or letters which say,
"He's not gone. He is just away with a jaunty wave and a
cheery smile."

It is tragic that in our cultural conspiracy to obscure the
reality and the finality of death we have missed the mysterious gift God has given to us. You know, the beautiful thing
is that there is death, and I believe it can be good. Illness
is sin, but death is a true gift of God not to be avoided. God
means for us all to pass through physical death; it's one of
his good gifts that we don't go on and on in this life. The late
Saul Alinsky, a secular prophet in our time and leading
organizer of the poor, once made this significant statement:
"The single most important thing I ever learned was that I
am going to die. For once you accept your own death, all of
a sudden you are free. You no longer care except so far as
your life can be used tactically to promote a cause you
believe in." When we have accepted the inevitability of
death, we can find a cause and say, "Lord, use me." Then
life begins. Somehow the acceptance of death is the beginning of life. People who are afraid to die have usually not
accepted either death or life.

Sometimes the theology of our time is written on the walls
of public buildings, and occasionally you'll discover profound truth in some rather unlikely places. Recently I came

across this sentence: "Death is nature's way of telling you to slow down."

Somehow the church of Jesus Christ needs to communicate this message: "Don't be afraid of death. Jesus is there. It's O.K." The important thing for each of us is to live life to the hilt. Eternal life begins now and death cannot interrupt its flow.

Examining the Institutions

Most major institutions in America are going through an identity crisis of enormous proportions. Not only are methods and resources being examined, but their very purposes, goals and unspoken assumptions are under intense scrutiny. I find this one of the most hopeful indications that these might be, in fact, the best of times rather than the worst of times. When we stop examining our production lines and question instead the product that comes off the ends of those lines, we may well expect some startling results in our national life.

For example, leading educators are not only grappling with unwieldy budgets, quality control, and, in the case of small colleges, shrinking enrollments; they are now questioning whether they even know what education is or ought to be, let alone how to provide it.

Leading psychiatrists and mental health experts are not only faced with poor facilities, inadequate staffs, and conflicting approaches to treatment, they admit that they are not really sure that they know what "mental illness" is any more, let alone how to treat it effectively. Some psychiatrists, like Thomas Szasz, teaching psychiatrist at Upstate Medical Center in New York, refer to mental illness as a "myth" and our overinstitutionalized treatment of it as a hoax perpetrated by unhealthy professionals who have their own pathology. This extreme view cannot be ignored in light of what recent testing indicates about the ineffectiveness of all major schools of therapy.

The most hopeful direction I see being taken by today's leaders in the field of penology is not a plea for larger and more modern prisons nor for more staff with longer credentials, but an attempt to redefine both crime and punishment, "criminals" and rehabilitation. With a published national recidivism rate of over 90 percent (more than nine out of ten released prisoners will return to prison) this quest for basics is most welcome, long overdue and fraught with hope.

Social work is going through the same kind of disillusionment with its strenuous efforts and minimal measurable results. A new definition of man and his predicament along with a reevaluation of what constitutes "help" on a person-to-person or state-to-person basis holds forth hope for the suffering in the days ahead.

Watergate has opened up the whole institution of government to inherent failures, inequities, and false assumptions that have existed as long as anyone living can remember. We now stand in that creative moment when we can say as a nation that we are not sure how true democracy ought to work and how the right persons can be found for elective office. We don't know how to insure honest and fair elections. We don't know how to be friends or allies without being patrons or policemen. These discoveries could lead to a rebirth of government by and for the people greater than anything ever imagined by our founding fathers.

Finally, it seems apparent that the church as an institution is losing ground as well. Most of the major denominations are losing members and financial support at an alarming rate. This very sobering fact could lead to a great spiritual renaissance where the churches and their leaders once again learn not to turn the wine of the gospel into water and where the resources of God through his faithful followers will once again be made available to seeking people everywhere.

The Beginning of the Christian Era

All of this is either bad news or good news—the worst of times or the best of times—depending upon your point of view. Personally I find encouragement in the idea that if the major institutions are really depleted, then we can begin again. We can say, "At last! We must be in for the greatest renaissance of all time." There's no need to kick these straw dogs down; they are collapsing. And if the people of God can come up with some fresh, workable alternatives, we might find that we are in the beginning of the Christian era. Perhaps up until now we have been in a pre-Christian era. Obviously the things we've done so far aren't working too well.

What are some of the remedies, some of the basic truths to nurture and to communicate clearly? A recent sociological study sheds some light on this, I think. Three cultures in which people normally lived to be about one hundred fifty years old, often as couples, having a sex life until the very end, were studied to see what they have in common. One is in Pakistan, one is in Russia, and the third is in South America. Though they have different climates, geography, and diet, all three cultures have discovered the gift of intimacy. Somehow the people in them are able to share who they are and to care about each other. They are intimate with many people, not sexually, but in relationships where they feel known and loved.

Now I find this fascinating for a number of reasons. One is in the parallel with the early Christian model. The overwhelming impression that must be received from a reading of the New Testament is that the life, death, resurrection, and coming in the Spirit of Jesus Christ at Pentecost created a society of believers. These early Christians were far from perfect in their "life together," as the New Testament records over and over. But they did have "all things in common." They were intimately related to Jesus Christ and to one another. Loving intimacy is the mark of life in the kingdom of God.

But while we may be ready on a global scale for the Christian era, I find that secular prophets like Ivan Illich are dreaming of "the convivial society"—a society where goods and products and property are less important than a national or global life-style that improves the quality of our life together. The possibility of people relating more meaningfully in the years ahead seems to be more important to the secular dreamers than people owning more goods and having more luxuries.

Cultivating Intimacy

If that's true, how can the church help us find intimacy? If you have a fight with your wife, can you share it in your church? If you're about to lose your job or you're drinking too much or you're afraid of death, can you go to your church and share these problems? Jesus said, "I came that you might have life." And that means eternally and now. It means physically and spiritually. There is death at the end, yes, but God planned for us to have a long life without illness, and somehow that's tied, sociologists are discovering, to intimacy.

What did Jesus do when he launched his kingdom? He took a dozen people and lived with them intimately for three years. They traveled around. (If you really want to know people, try traveling with them. See how they handle delays, lost luggage, poor accommodations.) The disciples knew each other. Countless days were spent together walking hot dusty roads, with no Holiday Inn on the horizon. They shared both feasts and fasts, eating in unlikely places with unorthodox people. They were free to jockey for position, to be resentful, tired, petty and jealous and to say so.

Some time ago I was involved in a workshop where the leader suggested we pair off, male and female, and role-play that we were married. Each of us was supposed to be having an affair. We were told not to reveal this to the other. For fifteen minutes we played these roles and at the end of that time the leader asked, "How do you feel?" Almost every person in that room began to report on a physical pain. Some said, "The longer this went on, the tighter my chest got." Or, "I developed a lump in my stomach." Or, "My whole left side began to get paralyzed."

This exercise made it apparent to all of us that the lack of intimacy, induced in this case by the need to cover up and deceive, can result in ultimate physical breakdown. In the intimate society dreamed of for the future, perfection may elude us, but we can strive for honesty, openness and acceptance. Just imagine what this could mean in the whole area of national health and preventive medicine.

Newness versus Goodness

That leads to another basic truth we need to communicate if we are to build the new society we seem so anxious for: *newness is better than goodness.* Somehow the church has tried to sell us on being good, on not sinning. Well, I'm not for sin and I don't believe God is either. But there is something more to life than the absence of sin. Martin Luther said, "Love God and sin boldly." Luther was not talking about license. He was not implying that because Christ died

for us on the cross, we can go out and do what we want. I
think this is what he was really saying: "If you believe
Christ died for you, you will worry less about your goodness because it is all taken care of. You can get about the
business of risky living, of putting your life into causes
where you may get ground up, where you will be misunderstood, where you may even get dirty because that's the
name of the game. If you sin, repent and back off and know
it's okay. The more important thing is that your life be
invested in a cause you believe in."

What is newness? The Bible promises that if any man be
in Christ he is a new creation. A friend tells me the Greek
word used for new in this case is "fresh," as in fresh bread.
So, the opposite of the life Christ gives you is to be stale,
not bad. Badness and goodness are not ours to have or give.
God will make us good in his own way, in his own time,
though it might take some of us a thousand years to make
it. We've got plenty of time if we really believe in eternal
life. But the thing which is ours to receive now by choice
is freshness and newness.

Changing the Structures

Well, if we are living in a time when so many of our
structures are crumbling, perhaps it would be helpful to
examine what they were built for in the first place. I heard
an educator say, "Let's face it. The PTA is one of those
structures we have built to keep parents out of the schools."
What about the structures we build physically or organiza-
tionally in the church? Do they help people get in touch
with God or do they keep people from meddling in the
church's business? Do we build structures to get people in
touch with themselves and God or to provide busy work for
some of God's people?

Somehow we've been conned into thinking that the structures of our time should remain unchanged. But experts are telling us there are two ways to approach the future, the linear way and the systemic way. The linear way proposes that if we know where we have been, we can draw the line on the graph and determine where we are going to be in three, four, five, or ten years—where we've been, we will be, only more and better or less and worse, depending on the direction of the graph. But the point is, the future is locked in and predetermined by the past.

In the systemic approach we can also graph where we have been, but it allows us a number of spinoffs or alternative futures. It's good indeed to know that our future doesn't have to be determined by our past. David Morrison, one of the senior teaching psychiatrists at Menninger's, says, "Fantasy, not reality, will determine what you and I do." In other words, our individual lives and our corporate life in America or the world will not be determined by the hard facts of reality, but by how we interpret reality—the fantasies, or as the Bible says, the dreams and the visions. The Christian church began at Pentecost when the prophecy was fulfilled that the young shall see visions and the old dream dreams. The people of God are dreamers who know that the things we fantasize—which are perhaps God's dreams in us—have the power to shape, predict, and direct our future. We are not locked in. And God seems to say, "Dream holy fantasies. Because the dreams that I can give to you about your own life, the life of your church, your town, your society, or your world will shape the future more than the facts revealed in the graphs of where we have been."

Society can change if we are people who are pro-active and not re-active. Most of us react to what has been—lovingly or unlovingly. But better than reacting lovingly is to pro-act—to get the dream and to initiate. Say, "God, show me what I can be in my home, in my school, in my town. Jesus, let your mind come into me."

A powerful message comes from Ecclesiastes 9:11: "The race is not to the swift, nor the battle to the strong, nor bread to the wise, nor riches to the intelligent, nor favour to men of skill; but time and chance happen to them all" (RSV). Can you believe that? Those with Ph.D.s and those who are smart and who run fastest aren't always going to make it. But you and I who have been passed by in education or skills or money or physical advantages can have something that the Spirit of God can work with—and that's hope. Hope that God gives us about what is and what can yet be.

What can be? I think Teilhard de Chardin said it best, "Some day after we have mastered the winds, the waves, the tides and gravity we will harness for God the energies of love and then for the second time in the history of the world man will have discovered fire." *

----
*Pierre Teilhard de Chardin, *On Love* (New York: Harper and Row, 1967), pp. 33–34.

3. THE THREE R'S—READIN', 'RITIN', AND RELATIN'

LIKE MOST of society's institutions, education both secular and sacred is in for a change, and this change is long overdue. Many of us are products of some of the worst of the old days, educationally speaking. But even if you are younger and are the product of schools a little less rigid and archaic, you still have to deal with people who came through the old school. It seems to me that public education heretofore has been based on some erroneous assumptions.

Learning is Difficult

One of those assumptions we operated with when I was in grade school and high school was that learning is very difficult. The idea seemed to be that if you have a high I.Q. and if you apply yourself and if you have a good teacher, you just might learn something. But if there's a deficiency in any one of those areas, you've had it for life. Of course, this isn't actually true. The schools—church and secular—try to make it hard, but learning is a natural process and actually ought to be easy.

41

Many people have carried reading blocks right on into
adulthood. They may have high I.Q.'s and now be heads of
industry or presidents of the Junior League, but can't read
or read very slowly and painstakingly. In all probability,
they suffered a reading block because it was drummed into
them, "Reading is difficult." When that idea fastens itself
in your mind, you reason, "I'm not smart." Convinced that
you can't read, you never read.

Learning Takes Place in School

My generation grew up with a second questionable assumption, that education or learning must take place in
school. Just as we believe that you've got to be in church to
be holy, we insist you've got to be in school to learn. If
you're not in school, you're not learning. And so we keep
attendance records and track down the truants.

Actually, I can't remember a great deal of what I learned
in my early years in school. My father consistently encouraged me to play hooky. I'm the only child of a second
marriage and, as I have said, my father was sixty when I
was born. By the time I was ten he was seventy. Life and
success were getting a little beyond him, but he was thrilled
to have a young son and spent much of his time with me.
That's a gift I couldn't give my children since I was young
and fearful and ambitious when they were growing up. To
my mother's horror (she was a former schoolteacher) he
would take me out of school and we would go to rodeos and
circuses, or fishing and kite-flying in the forest preserves
around Chicago. Once a month we would go down to the old
Rainbow Fronton in Chicago and watch the professional
wrestling matches. When we arrived home around mid-
night, mother would say, "The kid will be no good for
school tomorrow. How can you do this to a ten-year-old?"

Then, too, I'd go to his business lunches and his Kiwanis affairs where I learned about people and relationships, power and politics, and life in general. Let me assure you that learning takes place all the time! My father was equipping me for life—and it was fun.

Mastering Content

A third assumption from the "old days" was that content is the most important thing in education. That's really why we were in school—to master a particular body of knowledge. But content isn't the most important thing. It's more important to know where to find facts, how to make use of the library, and how to do research. A friend of mine is about to publish some research he has done which indicates from many controlled tests that highly educated people cheat more than less educated people, that smart people cheat more than stupid people, and that church members cheat more than nonchurch members. Why? I don't really know and neither does he. I would venture a guess that since our schools have exhorted us to get those facts, and since they reward us for those facts, we will do anything to get them, even cheat.

Trusting the Educational Elite

A fourth assumption was that there is an elite group of people somewhere in some great educational brain factory who know what the subject matter ought to be in order to produce educated people. When I went to high school I took a college preparatory course which included Latin. I had tutors all the way through those three years of Latin and mother took a part-time job to pay the tutor's bill. Why Latin? Because, "You've got to know Latin to be educated."

No wonder we have so many medical doctors and Catholic priests around. They can't waste the Latin they spent so many years acquiring. I, not being a priest or a doctor or a pharmacist, haven't used my Latin in thirty-five years.

Algebra was another important part of the required subject matter and, I was told, you've got to have this to get through college and through your life beyond college. Today with a little box on every desk that always comes out with the right answer when you push the right buttons, who needs algebra? Obviously, some people in special fields do have to have it, but I've never used mine. But somehow we have this implicit trust in an unseen group of people who decided what "education" was.

It is just that kind of trust that was implicit in our thinking during wartime. We assumed our cause was always just and those of us who were eligible served happily in the armed services. More recently some young people said, "We don't believe in this war, and we don't intend to fight." In the same way, some are beginning to have the courage to say, "We don't believe in the present curriculum in our schools." But when I was in school you didn't question curriculum. You just endured it because somebody somewhere knew what you ought to know for life. Today, in our complex society, the whole idea that someone can tell you what you need for life seems somewhat ludicrous.

Training and Education Make a Teacher

We also assumed back in our school days that special training and education qualified you as a teacher; eventually you got tenure and taught indefinitely. Well, I can think of many qualified teachers who stomped all over us. Now, as a neophyte moving around educational circles, I hear men like Arthur Combs, head of the education department of the

University of Florida, saying, "There are just two things
that teachers need and we can't really teach these two things.
The teacher must love himself or herself and the teacher
must love the students." This is a radical departure from
tenure and credentials. If you don't love yourself, you project that in the classroom, stifling students and inhibiting
them. If you love the kids, you create a climate that encourages learning.

School Is a Grading System

The sixth wrong assumption was that your school performance indicated your place in society. Graduates saved
their yearbooks to see who did what because performance
in school was an indication of your rightful place in life. It's
a grading system for all of us. Your school record is a per-
manent brand that you wear on your forehead as you go
through life. A new breath of freedom came when Erik
Erikson, one of Freud's great disciples, suggested that Freud
was wrong. We are not trapped by childhood. We can transcend our childhood and we can become something that we
never dreamed of in our childhood. I would add that we can
also transcend inadequate education, but many of us are
still struggling to do this.

I recall so well my frightening experience with music in
the first grade. My teacher said, "Bruce, you're a monotone.
You don't do badly for a monotone, but you are a monotone. So please keep still when the class is singing. It might
even help if you sat way over there." And do you know that
at heart I really am a marvelous singer. My wife will not
agree. But, two weeks ago we worshiped in a strange church,
and I had one of the great moments of my life when a lady
turned around after the service and said, "Oh, it's wonderful
to sit in front of somebody who sings as well as you do, sir."

(My wife is convinced that that lady is also a monotone!) Well, I'm usually off key, but what I lack in key, pitch or quality I supplement with volume, and there are moments in the shower when I rise to great heights. But I have been scarred for life by a teacher who said, "You're a monotone," and who put me in a corner so I wouldn't mess up the rest of the kids in the class. I have never outgrown that experience.

In second grade, another teacher said, "Bruce is the finest mathematician in our class if we let him count on his fingers." This statement sent the other students into fits of laughter as they all turned around and stared at me. To this day I am terrified of a column of figures. My wife does our income tax and our checkbook. But I have been certain for forty years now that I can't handle figures and I can't sing.

When I was in third grade we moved into a new school district. The school I had attended for the first two grades did not believe in teaching script until third grade; we printed. In my new school they were already writing. And there I sat, needing glasses (I had and still have about 20/200 vision). The teacher would ask, "Can you read this chart?" And I would say, "What chart?" (I thought it was a window.) I sat in that classroom almost blind and in any case unable to read writing. I was the new kid in class who couldn't read and couldn't see, who couldn't count and couldn't sing, and with a teacher named Miss Winkle whose every other remark was, "Bruce, I would like to throw you out the window!" Is it any wonder that the academic world has always intimidated me? I would rather be almost anywhere than "in school."

Now my mother is a real politician. During the early months of this terrible harassment, she went often to the school to complain, but it didn't help. Finally, she suggested that my father ought to go see my teacher. My father may

have been elderly but he was full of sex appeal, and the day
he came to school was another of those days when I began to
learn about the real world. At about ten o'clock one Monday
morning he arrived at the school and came to the door of my
classroom with Miss Hesselbaum, the principal. They called
Miss Winkle out of class. She was gone for over an hour.
I'll never know what happened, but from then on I became a
very special student to Miss Winkle and she frequently re-
marked about what a charming father I had.

School, the Great Conditioner

Well, let me suggest one final thing in this group of erroneous assumptions: School exists to indoctrinate you into
"the system"—the American way of life. In school you find
your fraternity or your sorority and you go through your
social puberty rites. But most of all you learn how to
fit in and where. In a discussion with John Holt, one of the
revolutionary educators of our time, he decried the fact
that so many firms hire only college graduates for executive
positions. Holt said he asked the personnel manager of one
firm if he really believed that applicants needed four years
of college to do the jobs they were being hired for. "Of course
not," was the answer. "Actually the jobs we are offering are
so boring and dull that we feel only those who have survived the tedious routine of college will stick with them. If
they haven't been through that conditioning experience they
will come in here and rebel and start making trouble for
us."

But even with all these wrong assumptions, a liberating
word came through to me from a high school teacher in
Evanston, Illinois. She was large, single, and elderly, and
she loved boys. When I came on the scene in my freshman
year, she made me her project. And under her guidance I

began to believe I was somebody. We never talked about
God, and I don't know anything about her faith. But through
that one teacher, God began to undo eight years of pure
educational hell.

An Authentic Educational Product

Beyond the effectiveness of curriculum and teachers and
buildings, it seems to me we have a very basic question:
What product are we aiming at educationally? Literate citizens? Well-balanced and wholesome citizens? Creative and
resourceful citizens? Perhaps we can't answer this question
without doing so in theological terms. To me, it seems man is
struggling for wholeness, to find all he is meant to be as a
person. This is so much bigger than academics and yet
something which could be aided and encouraged by the right
kind of educational system.

Fritz Perls, in speaking of wholeness, said, "For a person
to be whole there must be the continual possibility of four
important explosions; anger, joy, grief, and orgasm." If you
can't get angry, you're not whole. If you can't celebrate and
yell "Whoopee," you're not whole. If you can't cry when
you're hurt or your loved one dies or when babies are starving, if you can't express real grief and love, you're not whole.
If you are unable to reach releasing climactic sexual experience from time to time, you're not whole. (The point I
think Perls makes is that one need not actually experience
orgasm to be whole. But one is crippled if one is incapable
of experiencing sexual orgasm.) Education, especially Christian education, it seems to me might be aimed at helping
people to live fully in these four dimensions.

Carl Jung describes wholeness as the vital balance between
the conscious and the unconscious, giving equal recognition
to both. He said, "If you're too much one or the other you're

not whole." God gave us two sides to our brain; one is the unconscious and the aesthetic and the other the conscious and the practical. These need to be put in balance.

Dr. Elizabeth Kübler-Ross, who has researched death, spoke about wholeness and what is basic to wholeness in a talk I heard in Maryland. She says, "[It is] the ability to give and receive. Most of us are either givers or receivers. And the tragedy of old age is that people in nursing homes and hospitals are only allowed to receive." Receiving the best of care and loving-kindness is not enough for life. She suggests that nursing homes could be places where free day-care centers could be conducted for children of working mothers by the residents, who would then have the joy of feeling useful and needed once again. Nursing homes and retirement homes ought to be places of ministry, not just places for ministry. Question: How can the schools help all people, both young and old, begin to become both givers and receivers?

Dr. Thomas Szasz, teaching psychiatrist and author of *The Myth of Mental Illness,* gives an indictment of modern medicine which seems to apply to education, psychology, and the church as well. In a talk to a medical school graduating class recently, he said, "Fellow doctors, let me suggest to you something that is not always apparent to young doctors. For some people, a great many people, dignity is more important than health. If you dehumanize your patients and put them in situations where they are going to be dehumanized as people, they would rather die than receive your medical ministrations. Until you recognize the need most people have for dignity, you can't treat them."

Educators, church and secular, need to take this need for dignity seriously. In a recent survey, 90 percent of the students in one of the finer school systems said in an interview that they felt unimportant to the school and they were not included in decisions. When students feel unimportant, they lose interest in the whole educational process. All they need to do is stop coming and the schools would be forced to close. The students really have tremendous power in the school system. Beyond that, when they are in school, if they are continually minimized or ignored, their dignity is taken away and something irreparable happens which affects their lives for all time. (Maybe this also explains why so many of the organized churches are in trouble today.)

Learning to Be and Relate

What then of the goals of all education, secular and Christian? We're finally being forced to the conclusion that life is not mastering facts, not controlling things. This whole culture of acquiring knowledge and power over things is showing signs of a corporate disorganized personality (or nervous breakdown). We're beginning to realize that life, in a relational society, is basically "being." It's being and relating. These are the eternal, these are the real, and everything else is background. The whole material world is a background to what we are as people in our being and in our relating.

In this being and relating, we are unique individuals. And education for so long has been aimed at students' mastering predetermined bodies of content, regardless of their individual uniqueness. Everyone "must have" gym or science or shop. Certainly in one sense we are all alike. Obviously, there is a part of each of us that is universal. Part of you is just like me. You are lonely and I am lonely. When your kid is smoking pot or when you're threatened by your mate or your job or by illness, your fear feels like my fear. Your hope is like my hope and your joy is like my joy. Somehow as we begin to find that out we discover that we are brothers. Anybody in the people business—all good communicators, preachers, and educators—make use of their common humanity to build a bridge to others.

But on the other hand, there is the mystery of personality: I am not just like you. Knowing me doesn't mean I know you, because there is a part of you that I will never understand. God made you and threw away all the blueprints. Unless that unreproducible miracle that is your personality is allowed to emerge, you become like everybody else. You're one of a number of people all in the same school or sorority or club or church—all smelling and looking alike and marching to the same tune. Surely authentic Christian fellowship in any given tradition ought to enable me to become different from you and to affirm my uniqueness.

One psychiatrist has told us the neurotic says, "I wish I were Abraham Lincoln." And the psychotic says, "I am Abraham Lincoln." And the well person says, "I'm glad I'm me and I'm glad you're you."

A fascinating person lives near me who seems to be reveling in his uniqueness. His name is Vander Carr and he is an artist, a one of a kind in what he produces and in how he lives. He built a weird house of plaster forms and surrounded it with statues of witches. From time to time he runs an ad in the classified section of our paper. One said, "Girl wanted, seven foot seven, to pose for tall statue." A week later, "Instructions in modesty by world genius." Or, "Free cruise to Bahamas. Bring your own oar." All are simply signed Vander Carr. About a month ago he advertised, "For sale. Used time machine." It was later discovered some guy drove three hundred miles to buy it and found he was being sold an old alarm clock. In a newspaper interview, Vander Carr volunteered that his creed in life is to avoid the fool catcher. Further, he said, "I've got to get people interested in me."

Although his goals may be different, Vander Carr has a

lot to teach us about the kinds of people that ought to be produced by our educational systems. As a Christian educator, I have always lamented the fact that Christian education continually seems to lag behind secular education in method and technique. I rejoice that both are now going through a revolution. If our new goals are to help people become what they are meant to be, then, for once, the Christian church might be the advance guard for the relational revolution to come in all of education.

4. THE REVOLUTION IN THE CHURCH

THIS IS AN apocalyptic time—one in which those of us in the Western world and in America are trying to sort out our priorities and commitments. To what are we committed? What are the ultimate values for which we will trade the lesser values?

Not too long ago a Japanese lieutenant emerged from the Philippine jungles where he had been hiding out for twenty-eight years. He surrendered only after receiving personal assurance from the Emperor and his own general that the Second World War was over. This story produced conflicting reactions all over the world. Younger people regarded him as a fossil from a former age. Others said, "Whatever happened to the good old days when people defended causes they believed in, long after they were lost, for the sake of duty, honor, and country?" The lieutenant's unwavering commitment made him a cultural dinosaur to some and a hero to others.

Sorting Our Commitments

Most of us crave certainty. But, from all outward appearances, so many of us these days seem to lack a vital sense of commitment. An old friend of ours was an interesting gentleman. He was a wealthy, self-made man, living in an enormous old house in the suburbs. He drank perhaps a quart of the very best liquor every day and chain-smoked cigarettes. Three years ago his doctor said, "If you don't stop smoking and drinking, you will be dead in six months." Without hesitation he replied, "Doctor, I would rather live one day smoking and drinking than sixty years without." He died two months later.

This man knew what was important to him. His values were questionable, but they were definite. Most of us envy people who have certainty in their lives, even though in some cases it leads to rather bizarre results, as it did for the Japanese lieutenant.

It is interesting to observe, though, that we are guilty of a certain amount of hypocrisy in the commitments we do make. Even though we glibly proclaim our commitment to God, country, truth, a close look at our behavior often contradicts what we say. Recently a test was conducted at Princeton Theological Seminary and reported in the magazine *Human Behavior*. Forty students were selected for the test and separated into two groups. The students in the first group were told that a career study was being conducted. They were instructed to go as a group to a recording studio where each student would give a talk about his future career and his idea of ministry. The assignment for the second group was to go to the same studio and make a tape recording on their interpretation and understanding of the Good Samaritan story.

Unknown to the students, a professional actor had been

hired to stage an act for them as they walked along the route from the dormitory to the recording studio. As the students passed by, he clutched his heart and gasped, "Oh, this is the big one." With that, he toppled over. Sixty percent of the students didn't stop. They trudged right on to keep their appointments with the tape recorder. The article commented, "Some who were planning their dissertation on the Good Samaritan literally stepped over the slumped body as they hurried along. Interestingly, there was no significant difference in compassionate behavior between those who had the parable on their minds and those ready to talk about their future careers." What does that say about the Christian cause! No wonder the world is not impressed with our commitment.

Since the beginning of the twentieth century, one of our primary commitments as persons and as a nation has been the accumulation of money. This is especially true since the depression of the 1930s. We seem to have developed a passion for making money. But now the value of money in our inflationary society is being questioned. People are investing in material goods: jewelry, paintings, gold, land. Perhaps we are entering a post-money time—a time when bigness and growth and the accumulation of material things are seen as bad. Even now we are no longer witnessing the burgeoning industrial growth that made America the great polluting colossus it is. Hopefully, we are beginning to try to develop a quality of life instead. Certainly many of the under-thirty group seem militantly committed to that goal, with their homemade bread, organic vegetables, simple clothing, and cabins in the woods.

David Neiswanger of the Menninger Foundation says, "If each of us can be helped by science to live a hundred years, what will it profit us if our hates and fears, our loneliness and our remorse will not permit us to enjoy them? What use is an extra year or two to the man who kills the time he has?"

Let's face it, a hundred years of beer and television isn't a very exciting or fulfilling prospect. But if I am committed to a cause I believe in, then an extended life has meaning. And that's precisely what the church can give to people: a reason for living and a style of living that comes from belonging to Jesus Christ and participating in his grand design for the world.

Commitments are being reshuffled on the national scene today. Countries who in the past received massive aid from the United States are making new commitments and alignments, regardless of what we think or feel. Freedom and independence are more important to them than financial security. This ties right in with the conclusions by many psychiatrists that we all hate dependent feelings and ultimately will avoid people who do too much for us. If this is true, some pretty important questions are raised: How are the haves to treat the have-nots? How should parents treat children? How should we treat our wives or husbands? If people hate to be dependent, how are we to love and do for them without creating feelings of dependence?

But the opposite of dependency is freedom—something we all strive for. Sidney Harris, Chicago columnist, writes "that the liberty most men clamor for is merely the right to remain enslaved to the prejudices they have grown comfortable with. Genuine liberty to become who you are is more feared than coveted." Isn't that an amazing statement? Yet, this is exactly what the church has to offer in Jesus Christ, the freedom to become what he meant us to be. In a sense, that is a frightening thought, because this kind of freedom implies life without boundaries—an adventure into the immeasurable unknown with Christ. What a contrast to our daily "freedom" to read the same old papers and think the same stale thoughts!

A Time for Change

The growth boom of the church which occurred in the 1950s and early 1960s is faltering. The majority of the major denominations are in serious trouble: their overseas work is disappearing, national boards are shrinking, budgets are drastically sliced, church publications wallow in financial trouble or are buried, and inner-city parishes are dwindling and decaying. It appears to me that the structure of the church as we have known it is crumbling fast, and I say, "Hurray." The God of the church and the people of God will be here until the last days and beyond. But those structures which for the most part have done so little with so much seem to be going. On the other hand, when we describe the state of the church, it is a bit like describing Noah's Ark. It might smell and leak, but look at the alternative. How else can you survive the flood? We can't dump the church—we *are* the church. If we don't like what's happening—the forms, the structures, most of all the unreality—we must continue to be the people of God through whom new structures come about.

You and I, under God, can become architects of change. But we must remember that change isn't always welcomed, especially by the church. A wise word on that comes from the Menninger Clinic: "All of us on the staff (nine hundred people) are convinced that *all* change is experienced by *all* people as loss and is followed by anger." That insight from a group of psychiatrists helps us to understand the hostility people feel when confronted with change. It doesn't matter if the changes are good. People inherently do not like change and are angry when it comes.

My wife and I spent some time in California last year and, as always, I was intrigued by California citizens. I can't keep up their invigorating pace, but I love it. The day we arrived there was an article in the paper about a lady one hundred

years old who was divorcing her husband because he
wouldn't stop chasing girls, and he was one hundred and
three. Imagine! That could only happen in California. Obviously, here is a gal for whom it was never too late to
change! Now, I'm not plugging divorce, but this lady at one
hundred says, "I don't want this guy to wreck my life. If
the old codger is going to continue this hanky-panky, I'm
going to live my life without him. I'm not going to mess up
my remaining years."

How many of us feel stuck at fifty or forty or thiry-five?
You may say, "I wish I could have become a doctor, a dentist, a teacher, but it's too late. I can't go to college or graduate school." To believe at any stage that life is mostly over
and just "make do" with things as they are is no way to
live. With complete confidence in Jesus Christ we can dream
about the future and know that it's never too late. With
God in you, you can launch out and change. If you die the
next day, it's okay. I hope my wife will never divorce me,
because I love her with all my heart. But if one day she
feels that I am minimizing her or making her feel inferior or
in any way standing in the light that she needs to become
the person that God meant her to be, I hope she'll be free
to throw me out even if she's one hundred. There is something more important than our staying married, and it has
to do with integrity, personhood, and purpose.

A Time for Dreams

This is a time for dreams and visions and most of all for
hope. But remember, hope does not come from the facts.
Even though everything around you may seem to be crumbling and the fabric of society may seem to be falling apart,
it is possible this is the very time for building. Like the
Israelites who returned from captivity to find their home-

land in ruin, we may also have to start over to build a city or
a society under God the way he meant it to be. But we must
have dreams and plans. We've got to have something in
mind about how life can be different.

I have such a dream and I'd like to share part of it with
you. First of all, my dream is that we are coming into the
first days of the church. As I mentioned earlier, we could be
living right now in the beginning of the Christian era. I'm
not overly proud of church history from about A.D. 100 on.
True, in those first early years after Pentecost, something
earthshaking happened. But there has been so much done
since in the name of Christ that is shameful and painful:
inquisitions, crusades, witch burnings, massive indifference.

But maybe the dream that God gave the writers of the
New Testament about the church is going to continue now
in the twentieth century where it left off in the first. It's
possible. These could be the days referred to in John's Revelation:

> Then I saw a new heaven and a new earth; for the first
> heaven and the first earth had passed away, and the sea
> was no more. And I saw the holy city, new Jerusalem, com-
> ing down out of heaven from God prepared as a bride
> adorned for her husband; and I heard a great voice from
> the throne saying, "Behold, the dwelling of God is with
> men. He will dwell with them, and they shall be his peo-
> ple, and God himself will be with them; he will wipe away
> every tear from their eyes, and death shall be no more,
> neither shall there be mourning nor crying nor pain any
> more, for the former things have passed away (Rev. 21:1-4,
> RSV).

I must admit, though, my feelings that these are the "first
days" of the church are not actually based on facts. Albert
Camus said it well, "In the midst of winter I finally learned
that there was in me an invincible summer." In the midst of
darkness we can see blossoms and light. I can see the

springtime of the church, the almond shoot coming up amidst two thousand years of smoking slagheaps.

A Fellowship of Healers

In the Book of Acts we find this startling record about the first years of the church:

> Many miracles and wonders were being performed among the people by the apostles. All the believers met together in a group in Solomon's Porch. Nobody outside the group dared join them, even though the people spoke highly of them. But more and more people were added to the group—a crowd of men and women who believed in the Lord. As a result of what the apostles were doing, the sick people were carried out in the streets and placed on beds and mats so that, when Peter walked by, at least his shadow might fall on some of them. And crowds of people came in from the towns around Jerusalem, bringing their sick and those who had evil spirits in them; and they were all healed (Acts 5:12–16, TEV).

So, in its beginning days the church was known as the place where you could bring the socially, mentally, and physically sick. It's interesting to note that those healed weren't all Christians; many were unbelievers. Even the believers were a motley crew: some were gluttons and some drunkards and all had a rather shaky theology. But Christ was in them—making himself known to all by his power to heal through the Apostles.

What do people in your town say about the church? "They're nice folks." "They've got some funny ideas about God." "They get very emotional and jump around a lot." "They're gung-ho to clean up the slums, or close the bars, or to get you to their pancake supper or Christmas bazaar." Suppose people in your town could say, "I don't know about their theology, and I'm not even sure about their ethics—

they may not be much better than we are. But, if we can get that hopeless case over there to them, he might be healed, because God is with those people."

If this were true, God's people would be known to the world as a fellowship of healers. That once was true, and I know some places today where miracles in God's name still occur. This is not evangelism. It is pre-evangelism. It is not our choice to say, "Well, if you're a believer, we'll work with you." But rather, in the spirit of Christ and the early apostles, we are just to say, "Come." When this happens, the entire church can be a fellowship of healers, a royal priesthood—mediators of the healing and love and grace of God to people who are sick and in need.

An incident from many years ago sticks with me vividly: One of the kids at school took a magnifying glass out of his pocket and held it at just the right angle so that the rays of the sun could shine through it. In just a few moments the leaves in the pile on which the glass was focused burst into flame. I could not believe my eyes.

My dream for the church is that you and I will be that kind of magnifying glass—the means God can use to bring his fire into focus on the world. When that happens, people and events will be changed, as the grace of God through Christ unleashed the power of the gospel on the world two thousand years ago.

Jesus doesn't promise that we'll be especially good in this life, and most of us probably won't be particularly wise. But our lives can become a prism through which God's infinite love and power will shine, as we live intensely with another person—listening, praying, asking questions, giving of ourselves. I believe our lives are meant to be simple, uncomplicated magnifying glasses that focus God's power. We don't heal; God heals. There is no fire in the magnifying glass. When we as the church become this fellowship of healers through whom God heals, he will have a whole new kind of public relations in the world. This will not be some form of superevangelism, but people quietly going about being the instruments of healing for others.

When this happens, the "first days" of the church *now* will be like the first days of the church in the first century. God will be working in ordinary simple people doing profound miracles. Paul Tournier once said to me, "I'm convinced that nine out of ten people seeing a psychiatrist don't need one. They need somebody who will love them with God's love and take time with them and believe for them, and they will get well." This is our mandate. Carl Jung, the great psychoanalyst, was counseling a man who had been in therapy for six months and was getting no better. Finally Jung said, "Friend, I can't do any more for you. What you need is God."

"How do I find God, Dr. Jung?" the man asked.

"I don't know," said Jung, "but I suspect if you will find a group of people some place that believe in him passionately and just spend time with them, you will find God." The man did just that and he was healed.

A Fellowship of Riskers

I also dream that the church will become known as a fellowship of riskers. If we really have faith and hope and the ability to love with God's love, we are called to a life-style of risking. Is this the reputation you and I have with our peers? Do they say, "Oh, there's old crazy Bruce. He's always off on some new venture"? Jean Cocteau said, "You should find out what you can do best and never do it again. Because you should risk failure." Although using obvious hyperbole, this wise man is saying that the real test of life is found in your willingness to risk.

I'm always encouraged by the kind of risky living modeled by the Apostle Paul. When he was about to head for Jerusalem and then on to Rome, he was entreated by the saints not to go: "Paul, we need you, man. You are a prism, a magnifying glass for God. You are an encourager—our father in the faith. Don't go. They're going to get you in Jerusalem." But he replies, "What are you doing, crying like this and breaking my heart? I am ready not only to be tied up in Jerusalem but even to die for the sake of the Lord Jesus." They could not convince him so they gave up and said, "May the Lord's will be done" (Acts 21:12–14).

Where will your particular mission take you? I don't know what your personal vision is, but if you follow it all the way, "they" are going to get you too, right where you are vulnerable. You probably know the place: in your past, in your family, education, sports, military service, or in your denomination. Or someone in your present: your boss, competitor, your young assistant, your neighbor, your enemy or your best friend. But in my dream we are known as a fellowship of riskers. Our theology may be suspect and our goodness may not be worth much, but someone in the world may say, "You know, that bunch of Christians will risk anything as they care for others. I want to find out what motivates and enables people to live with that kind of reckless abandon."

A Fellowship of Nonconformers

Finally, the church will be known as a fellowship of people who are finding their uniqueness. Ideally, it is the only institution in all of society that is not trying to make its members conform. Almost without question every other group in the world—hippies, establishment types, conservatives, liberals, radicals, revolutionaries—has a distinctive com-

mon smell, look, and vocabulary. The pressure is to come
and join in being the same kind of nonconformists. Too often
the church is in the same trap. But we are meant to be a
fellowship of people bound first of all to Christ and then to
each other. As we live out this life in worship, prayer, study,
and mission, we are committed to the freedom of becoming
different from each other. Each of us is to become the unique
person only we can be under God.

Peter DeVries is one of my favorite novelists. The hero
in one of his recent books is Stu Smackenfeld, a second-rate
ham actor on Broadway and a man of great excesses in his
personal life. The plot sees him through many bizarre events.
Finally, on the last page of the book his wife turns to him
and says, "It must be very difficult to be Stu Smackenfeld."
And this fellow who has stepped in the mush about twenty-
seven times through the three hundred pages of the book
answers reflectively, "Yes, dear. And I'm not sure I'm right
for the part."

This is the primal cry. Who am I? Am I right for the part?
In one way or another each person seems to be saying, "I
want to find out who I am before I die." And the only way
we are going to discover that, I believe, is from God and the
fellowship of the church.

5. IDENTITY—
THE ULTIMATE
SEARCH

      LATE ONE night Hazel and I were driving through the mountains of Pennsylvania on a six-lane super-highway. As we rounded a bend in the road, we came upon a drive-in theater. And there on the huge screen, clearly visible from the highway, two people were engaged in sexual intercourse. It must have been a double X movie. Many cars had pulled off on the shoulder of the road to watch. There was no sound—but who needed sound?

To me this scene was a parable of America's present search for intimacy. Pornographic material which couldn't be purchased in a plain brown wrapper a few years ago could be viewed on a one-hundred-fifty-foot screen. It seems to me this trend indicates a tremendous hunger to gain a glimpse into the intimate lives of other people. Possibly this is one phase of our search for a clue to our own identity.

Americans have never been more aware of this ancient and primal search for identity. A friend of mine commented recently that he was going through an identity crisis and an energy crisis at the same time: "I don't know who I am and I'm too tired to find out."

We are witnessing a search for identity not just by individuals but by whole groups of people as well: blacks, teenagers, those in middle years, senior citizens, women. The women's libber, for instance, is saying among other things that she wants to be more than a wife or a mother or an unequally paid staff member. What she clamors for is to be a person. She is tired of the limiting stereotypes of womanhood which have been laid on her from childhood. A teacher friend once shared with me an essay defining people that a little girl in her class had written. "People are composed of girls and boys. Also men and women. Boys are no good at all until they grow up and get married. Men who do not get married are no good either. Boys are an awful bother. My mother is a woman and my father is a man. A woman is a grown-up girl with children. My father is such a nice man that I think he must have been a girl when he was a boy." This little girl's reverse sexism is readily apparent, and her identity as the female is closely tied with marriage, motherhood, and niceness.

But the quest for our true identity has been recorded from Genesis to Erik Erikson. To find out who you really are and to become that person is what The Great Adventure is all about. The most profound questions of all time are: Who am I? Where did I come from? What am I doing here? Where am I going? What does it all mean? Are you like me? Am I like you?

Who Am I?

The search begins very early in life, and it seems to me there are a number of areas in which our unique identity has traditionally been sought. Possibly, one of the most obvious is in our heritage. Virtually every newspaper carries an ad offering to help you trace your lineage and draw up your coat of arms. And one of the major complaints of blacks

is that they have been robbed of a sense of heritage. Black
studies courses have been instituted in most schools of
higher learning in a search for this lost heritage.

But many of us today who are not black share in the
same experience. Both of my parents were Swedish immigrants. After coming to the United States, they met, fell in
love, and were married. I've never seen either of their ancestral homes. I'd never met any of my relatives until very
recently. As a boy growing up, I didn't know what it was
like to have grandparents, aunts, uncles, or cousins. Perhaps
that's why I'm always so moved by that Coca-Cola television
commercial where they equate their product with "country
sunshine." In it we see a pretty girl climbing down off a
train and jumping into a creaky taxicab with old Charlie
the cabdriver. They drive to the farm and there are dad and
mom and the hired man and the cows and the boyfriend.
She's home! For me, the scene is very poignant because I
have no home. I have no place, no heritage. During my
growing-up period, in the midst of the depression, we moved
every two years to cheaper and cheaper lodging. And so today I'm still looking for my heritage.

Sometimes I find it in strange and unexpected places. On
one of my trips to New York City I visited the Oyster Bar in
Grand Central Station. This had been a familiar haunt of
mine twenty-five years ago when I was in seminary. Every
week on my way to filling a vacant pulpit in some small
church I would pass through Grand Central. I never failed to
stop in at the Oyster Bar for a bowl of oyster stew. As I
wandered in now, I found the same men serving the same
oyster stew in the same surroundings. At least they looked
the same: taciturn elderly men opening oysters and making
the stew right before your eyes. The somewhat ster-
ile décor was unchanged. It had always reminded me of a
large men's room. And the rich, penetrating aroma of the

oysters cooking in their own juice with a generous supply
of fresh butter still filled the place. Nothing had changed
but the price. It was like the country sunshine commercial.
I had come home. Yes, if we look hard enough, there are still
some things we can count on. For me the Oyster Bar at Grand
Central Station is one of them.

As we view the church today, it is helpful to realize that
for many people it fulfills this function. People who have
no homeland, no heritage, and who have been uprooted psy-
chologically or emotionally find security through worshiping
in a traditional fashion in a familiar building. This is sometimes hard on the minister. When I was in a parish preaching what I thought was a revolutionary gospel, calling on
everyone to attack the forces of evil and change the world,
I had little patience with people who were against change
in the church. I have since come to understand that many
find comfort in the fact that the church is the one unchanging part of their lives.

Picture with me, if you will, a man approaching fifty. His
marriage has never been particularly exciting. His children
put him down or ignore him. He has gone as far as he can
in his job and the work itself is dull and unrewarding. He
lacks the ability to make close friendships. His mother and
father are dead. Once a week for an hour, he sits in the same
church pew where he sat between his mother and father for
so many years. Here in quiet contemplation he can relive
that time of his greatest security when prospects were prom-
ising and he knew who he was. The customary order of
service, the familiar hymns and anthems, the remembered
stained glass windows, and even the musty smell of the
sanctuary provide an island of security once a week that
makes the rest of life bearable.

Now let's carry the picture a bit further. Imagine that a
revolutionary new minister comes into the sanctuary bring-

ing modern music and guitars. Some of the worshipers are long-haired and wear bib overalls or blue jeans. The minister encourages interaction in the pews or he may even take out the pews so the congregation can sit on the floor. Of course our middle-aged parishioner is opposed to that, and I can understand why. To him the familiar and the traditional represent God one hour a week. A preference for a wheezy old organ or off-key piano and hymns sung forty years ago may have nothing to do with musical tastes. Quite likely his mission in church, as in life, is to continue the search for his heritage.

Of course, unlike me, historically speaking, you may have a noble and aristocratic heritage. Your relatives may even have crossed on the *Mayflower*. But no matter how glorious the achievements of your ancestors, your heritage cannot ultimately provide your identity. Even the Apostle Paul deprecated his heritage. In words of today he said, "Nobody has a heritage like mine. You think you've got ancestors? Look at mine! You think you've got credentials? Look at mine! You think you're educated? Look at my diplomas!" He had the heritage to end all heritages and he insisted, "It is as nothing compared to finding out who I am in Jesus Christ."

Where Am I?

Others are trying to find their identity through the right environment, believing that living in the right place and with the right people around us we can become the persons we were meant to be. I'm often inclined to feel that if I could escape to some island paradise with none of the usual conflicts or failures or difficulties, I would become the mature person I am meant to be. However, some rather interesting tests have been conducted which seem to prove otherwise.

People have been placed in a situation as nearly lacking in environment as possible where they are weightless and can neither see, hear, smell, nor taste. Invariably, after about two hours, they break down emotionally. So it seems that our environment is actually a means by which we discover who we really are. To have only those people around us who react like soft cotton wool is to be without an environment. And to be surrounded by yes men is deadly. Actually, we find out who we are even from those who don't like us and who make life difficult for us.

Then, I suspect that the kind of multi-marriage patterns so common today represents in part this search for the right emotional environment. We have been programed to believe that with marriage to the "right person" our identity search is finally over. It is true that marriage is a great adventure. But you don't find out who you are just by getting married. Your mate, your children, or your best friends can't tell you who you are.

On the other hand, being a hermit or a bachelor is certainly not the answer. One definition of mental health is that it is the ability to tolerate inconsistency. We all must learn to tolerate all kinds of inconsistency in our environment. That is maturity. The story of Joseph in the Old Testament has a lot to say on this subject. He was so much at home with himself that he felt secure in any environment—even a hostile environment. Imagine, first of all he was the hated brother in the family. Then he lived as a slave in Egypt. Then through a series of amazing circumstances he became the number two man in Egypt—second only to the pharaoh. Eventually, the very brothers who sold him into slavery in the first place went to Egypt looking for food. They were terrified, but with no malice Joseph said, "You meant it for evil, but God meant it for good." This is a liberating concept for all of us. If we know who we are and whose we are, the worst environment can't hurt us. You needn't be a hermit. You can live right where you are and still be the person you were meant to be.

We are in trouble if we're looking only to our environment for clues to our identity. One Saturday I visited our neighborhood shopping center with my wife and found a huge army combat helicopter set up in the middle of the parking lot as a recruiting gimmick. I was intrigued and walked over to admire this awesome war machine.

"Are you interested in enlisting, Mac?" asked one of the lieutenants.

"Not really. I've put in my time," I said demurely. "I'm a veteran from quite a long way back."

He said, "Well, we want veterans. Let's talk about it."

"Well, I really think I'm too old," I finally ventured.

"You're not too old," he reassured me. "How old are you?"

"Forty-eight."

"Right on!" he said, "You are too old!"

Walking away, my wife said, "You surely love to have people think you're younger than you are." She's right. I do. And this is just the point. If by manipulation I can draw flattering responses from my environment, it's all too easy to conclude that my environment is supplying me with truth. But no matter how young those around me think I am, it doesn't change my true age one bit. In the same way I can get feedback that I am wiser or kinder or more talented than I am. But it doesn't change what I am.

One final observation. There isn't any one environment that is ideal for everyone. The environment maximum for me to grow and find my identity is not necessarily maximum for you. At Grace Hospital in New Haven, Connecticut, they have discovered there is no ideal environment for recovery in treating the mentally ill. Some people do better in private rooms, others in wards. Some thrive in austere conditions and others improve faster in very posh conditions. There is no single environment maximal to all.

Where Do I Belong?

Traditionally, we have also searched for identity in community. From the very first nursery school experience up through the more recent and sophisticated communes we seek to belong. But, community was elusive for me as a boy. We moved so often that I never really made it with any crowd. I was always the oddball, the last chosen, the new kid in town. And I used to ache for a group of people who would want me and love me and accept me just the way that I am—who would say, "It's O.K., Larson, whatever you are, you belong to us."

It seems to me that community comes the closest to being a genuine means of finding identity. Most of us want so much to know and be known and yet, for some strange reason, we choose to live in loneliness. The incident that best highlights this paradox for me took place when I was driving my motorcycle home from work on a four-lane highway one day. (I'm really over-age for a motorcycle and I feel a little embarrassed about it, so I always try to look like Joe Cool.) It was rush hour and the traffic was heavy—there was a car behind me, a car in front of me, and a panel truck was passing me on the left. Suddenly a wasp flew into the open front of my shirt. (That's a great argument for wearing neckties when you ride a motorcycle.) That rascal really began to give it to me with his stinger, but if you had been passing me at that moment, you wouldn't have known anything was wrong. Afraid I would panic the whole parade and have an accident, or, even worse, that I would look ridiculous, I continued to ride along looking pleasant and unperturbed. Before I could pull over conveniently and whip off my shirt on a side road, I had six wasp stings (by actual count later that night).

Now, all around us today there are people with wasps in their shirts who have chosen to look like Joe or Josephine Cool. They don't want to be embarrassed or to embarrass us, so they miss an opportunity for true community and belonging. The next time you are worshiping on Sunday morning, look around at all those spiritual types looking so devout and detached and reverent. Suppose you knew that wasps were stinging each of those people while the choir was singing or the preacher was preaching or we were all engaged in prayer. How would you react? How would you describe your own wasp stings? They could be the stings of a marriage where two people are engaged in mutual destruction with sulks, slights, or open hostility, or those sharp jabs of conscience when we have been indifferent or unfeeling. They could be the awareness that we have been drinking too much and don't know how to stop, or that we have been dishonest with our finances. They may be wasp stings of sexual fantasies or of actual affairs—stings of resentment or jealousy or fear. If needy people full of wasp stings could come together to affirm a belief in a God who loves and cares, who forgives and gives second chances, worship might be changed immeasurably.

In the true community, not only are our hurts taken seriously, but our fantasies and dreams as well. The theology of hope is important. Genuine hope is a gift of God out of which life-changing fantasies and dreams can come. I was delighted when the daughter of friends told me of bringing her very attractive and curvaceous blonde roommate home from college with her for the holidays. Introducing her friend to her grandfather, the girl added: "And just think, Jane, he's in his nineties." "Early nineties," the old gentleman corrected. Life-giving fantasies can keep us from ever growing old. It's

possible to die young in your nineties, and hope makes the
difference.

But fantasies can also change life for successful middle-
aged businessmen. A short while ago Hazel and I received
this letter from a new friend:

Dear Hazel and Bruce:
   You could surely tell from our telephone conversation
last week that I have finally found what I had been looking for after searching for it for the last ten or fifteen
years.
   It is so amazing because I have worked so long and so
hard, and felt that my prayers were not being answered.
As I told you I've always had such a deep biblical and
spiritual belief, but such a distant feeling from God. Mine
wasn't even a waving relationship, but a lost feeling of
where is he? A feeling I know he is there but where?
   Then my sister talked me into going to the Christian
Festival in Baltimore. Man, was I scared to go to Baltimore
and be among a group of pious, religious, praying, critical,
goody-goody Christians. . . .
   But within the first hour of the first night of sharing one
on one with a stranger I felt God touched me and gave me
new eyes with which to see myself and the world and him.
He also put new words into my mouth to help describe
what it was that I saw.
   What an experience! I felt set free! Before that I was a
believer but I couldn't perform. Something had been missing. I had that feeling of emptiness, pressure, and the need
to constantly work hard at everything I did. My whole
life was like trying to make love standing up in a hammock
—totally impossible! And the harder I tried the more impossible it became.
   [He then goes on to describe some of the changes in his
relationships at home and in business, in church and with
friends.]
   It's like I have been blind with my eyes and mind and
now I see people—almost everyone looks so real and
beautiful. I could go on and on but will keep notes of my
daily happenings and will write more some time later.

He *has* kept notes and the experience continues. He is living out his new life in a small group that studies, prays, and works to change life in that entire town for all the people. This is what authentic community is all about. It both calls forth fantasies and sustains people in their God-given fantasies about themselves and about what life can be for others around them.

For many years I have been in touch with two lovely sisters who are both missionaries in Africa. I cannot name them or their emerging country because of the many difficulties inherent there. Recently they wrote to tell me how discouraged they were at a government edict preventing them and all other missionaries from teaching the Bible in the public schools. But as the various missionaries prayed together about this new development, God gave them the gift of hope. They knew that this present circumstance would open new doors for the gospel. Listen to a paragraph from a letter that has just come:

> In January the government took over all of our schools which means there will be no more classes in religion even if we are allowed to teach in them. This is or will probably turn out to be for our good. At last our people are beginning to face up to the fact that part of the responsibility for getting Christ across to their children may be their own. They are starting to think of ways to strengthen our Sunday schools and some of the more advanced leaders are facing the fact that there must be some home teaching.

The longer I live the more I am convinced that one of the great gifts that God can give us in community is to have a sense of hope not based upon the realities around us. David Morrison at the Menninger Clinic was correct: fantasies shape the future more than facts. If I live my life alone or in the wrong kind of community I will become a victim of the facts. But with the people of God in true community holy fantasy will be a key that ever unlocks prison doors. If

I am to find my true identity I must find a community of people who will accept me and take my dreams and fantasies seriously.

What Do I Do?

From about age twenty-five on, a big part of our identity is defined by what we do, and even earlier it is shaped by what we plan to do. For years I looked for just the right job. I was convinced that if I had the right job I would know who I am. From the beginning, a man's identity has probably been more closely tied up with how he earns his living. A movie like *The Immigrants*, the story of early Swedish settlers in America, reminds us that for immigrants or pioneers the task was simply to stay alive, and it took all they had to do that. When they were engrossed with building a home to keep out the cold and raising or foraging for enough food to feed the family, they had no problems of identity. They were just trying to stay alive, fighting off Indians, bears, cold, and illness. Similarly many of us who were in the armed services remember those as great days because our identity was so clear. We knew who we were. We were part of a team out to fight another team, to win and save the world. But at home and back on the job we are faced with the age-old question again, "Who am I? What does it all mean?" And we search for the right kind of job or mission to answer this question for us.

Speaking in California just before he died, Abraham Maslow said, "The only happy people I know are those who are working hard at something they think is important." (*Not* something your spouse, friends, or parents think is important.) If *you* think that what you're doing is important, you have a beautiful edge on knowing who you are. At least for a time.

What Do I Know?

For another group, perhaps a smaller group, the quest for identity is closely tied to a search for wisdom. As a boy, I knew I would never make it as an athlete. When you have both uncoordinated muscles and baby fat well into high school you're in trouble. I played on the football team faithfully, but I was always the coach's last choice during the game. So while my friend next door was buying books by Charles Atlas, determined he wasn't going to be a ninety-seven pound weakling any more, I discovered the Rosicrucians. Their ads promised I would learn the mysteries of the ages and the knowledge of the wise men. That was for me! So I bought all of their material and began to read eagerly, sure that if I knew enough, I would know who I was and what life was all about. But I soon realized I wasn't going to make it on the wise men's team either. So I switched to the study of hypnotism, hopeful that this less esoteric and more direct approach to influencing people would work for me. No comment!

Surely a big part of wisdom is knowing your goal and pursuing it single-mindedly. I'm always impressed with the advice Pharaoh gave Joseph's brothers. He told them to bring their father and come to Egypt but to give no thought to their goods. Their future survival depended on leaving their material goods behind. Wisdom for you and me as well lies in knowing what to leave behind or to omit. Planned neglect is the secret of success. Less household chores and more practice makes a concert musician!

How do we sort out what is needed for life's journey? What things are negotiable and which can we lose only at great peril? Wisdom is knowing which things we can let go of happily and gladly without risking our identity or deflecting our true purpose. There are no courses in this kind

of wisdom. Actually, very few things are really necessary
for the journey, but which few are they? They vary for each
individual. That's what wisdom is all about and it can't be
mass-produced.

Our oldest son graduated from Northwestern University
in 1975. Walter Cronkite, the TV news analyst, received an
honorary degree during the ceremonies. Of the eight promi-
nent people being similarly honored, I noticed on the
program that he was the only one who had not finished college. Apparently Walter Cronkite decided early that a college degree was not essential in finding and fulfilling his
destiny as one of America's most powerful, influential, and
respected men.

It is always dangerous to read the success stories of other
people in order to look for a blueprint for your own success.
The quest for identity is tied up with the mystery of finding
my unique program and my unique priorities. No one else's
program will do for me. Erik Erikson, professor emeritus of
Harvard University, didn't find it necessary to have a high
school diploma. Albert Schweitzer left Europe and the world
of academia, the world of music and fine instruments, the
world of culture, to find his destiny in the most primitive
part of Africa. Martin Luther gave up the ecclesiastical ap-
proval of the Roman church to find his identity and destiny
as a priest of God. One of the most creative men I know of
today in the field of black education is a white man who
gave away a million dollars some years ago because it was
an encumbrance. Millard Fuller was a poor Southern boy
who had to earn his way through college. He earned so much
money "on the side" that shortly after he graduated his
accountant told him that he had a million dollars. But when
Millard found God, he discovered that his own personal future and his destiny depended upon his giving away that
very million. Since then he has helped black colleges, worked

with Clarence Jordan in Koinonia, Georgia, and is now a one-man crusade for faith and better living conditions in a number of places in Africa. In Fort Myers, Florida, where I now live, Thomas Edison maintained a winter home, a place where he did many of his most important experiments. You recall that this great American genius slept only two or three hours a night—the traditional eight hours was too much. The point is that no one formula for the journey of life applies to all of us. We must find by innate wisdom what is necessary for us and get on with it.

Can I Change Who I Am?

Since the turn of the century more and more people have been searching their unconscious as a means of finding their identity. Centuries before Freud, Jesus was the great explorer of the unconscious.

But while we owe much to Sigmund Freud for his exploration into the whole area of the unconscious, psychologists and psychiatrists today are rejecting much of his emphasis. There are probably a number of reasons why Freud is not popular today. First of all, he did not believe that you could transcend your childhood. Today, with the work of men like Erikson, we have come to believe we can transcend childhood. Second, Freud laid much emphasis on the unconscious and assumed we had access to it. This, too, is questioned today. Third, Freud emphasized the telling of your history to another as a means of understanding who you are and as a means of gaining access to your unconscious. Today psychologists believe that your personal history is unreliable, for we all unconsciously write and rewrite our history to suit our own purposes. Finally, many present-day psychologists, therapists, and psychiatrists are urging patients to stay in the now rather than dredging up the past. They avoid

the question "Why?" and instead ask "What?" and "How?"
The reason *why* you are in a situation is not relevant. To
understand *what* the situation is and *how* you can get out of
it are more creative questions, according to these present-
day therapists.

Let's see how this new approach works. McClean and At-
kinson did tests with children which demonstrated the power
of our unconscious. They gave a group of five-year-olds some
quoits, those round rope loops, with instructions to throw
them onto a peg. Some of the children would go over to the
peg and just drop the rings on it, scoring a bull's-eye every
time. That approach is used by the defeated child. He figures
that is the only way he can win.

Other children stood so far back they couldn't possibly hit
the peg. They threw the quoits for hours with no hope
of winning. This is another example of the defeatist attitude
of those programed to fail. They either say, "I'm no good
and won't even try" or they tackle jobs so big and difficult
they can't possibly succeed. In their unconscious they don't
want to succeed. Children who could stand at a reasonable
distance and throw the quoits, winning some of the time
and having the fun of winning, were those with a healthy
attitude toward achievement and tasks. The study proved
that even at five years of age, some people simply cannot
handle winning. When you begin to understand the forces
in you that are saying, "Don't win," or "Don't try," or "You're
inferior," or "You're really superior," then you are making
inroads on the search for identity we're talking about.

Now, suppose someone using this new therapy that mini-
mizes the importance of causes was working with those
children already programed to fail. He would not ask them
why they were acting as they were; he would ask rather if
they wanted to win and then suggest how they might change
their behavior to have the fun of occasionally winning.

The Good News

In my own search for identity, I find that the most relevant factor in the life equation is Jesus Christ and the fact
that he has a plan and a purpose for my life and the lives
of the people around me—that we might become everything
we are meant to be. This may mean finding the right environment, the right goal, the right community, the right
job. But basically it is in the relationship of love that we
begin to dance the dance of life and find our true function.

In this search for identity the gospel gives the deepest answers I've found to individuals, personally and corporately.
The gospel is Good News at all levels of life. It is cosmic, it
is personal, it is medical, it is social, it is educational, it is
psychological.

6. THE REVOLUTION IN THEOLOGY— RELATIONAL THEOLOGY

TRAVEL IN different countries across the world is an exciting and rewarding experience. But I have become increasingly fascinated by the idea that if you really are to enjoy it fully, a frame of reference is required—some structure with which you personally can identify.

For example, Dr. Clement Bowers, a botanist friend from Cornell University, once made an extended trip throughout Europe. He experienced each country through the eyes of a gardener, a botanist, and his beautiful colored slides focused almost entirely on the lush, well-manicured gardens.

I've known other people who toured Europe to visit the cathedrals, examine church organs, eat exotic cuisine, collect art. People travel for many different reasons—even though many just seem to meander aimlessly from one city or country to the next. But I'm convinced that if a person travels with some screening grid or sorting device, the trip will take on much greater meaning.

So it is with life. To understand and process the data we get from life, one needs some frame of reference, an interpretive structure—a theology. All of us are theologians—some are professionals, but most of us are what a friend of mine calls "natural" theologians. Both kinds are equally valid. Happily, theology is not the exclusive property of the professionals. It is simply a view of God and life. And consciously or unconsciously, we all have a grid of reality or certain markers by which we sort out and try to understand what we see.

It seems to me that more and more people have developed an awareness of this truth in the past ten years. This is the climate in which relational theology has emerged. In the late 1960s we began to realize in a new way that life centers in relationships and the Kingdom of God is in truth the kingdom of right relationships. Jesus said, "I came that you might have life and have it more abundantly. . . ." To have a full, or abundant, life means being reconciled by the cross in the four major relationships of life: to God; to one's self; to significant others (family, immediate friends and colleagues); and to the world (the rest of humanity whom one can choose to love or ignore). To put it simply and personally, Jesus came as Savior so that through his love and sacrifice I might be able to love God, myself, the significant others in my life, and the world (or some specific part of it) in a meaningful way.

Since relational theology emerged at the same time in history that the human potential movement was born and spread like an epidemic, many people have viewed this approach to theology as "humanistic" and not really biblical. Rather, those of us most identified with relational theology feel that it is in fact an attempt to return to biblical theology.

The precise point and purpose of the incarnation was to reconcile God and man—to enable a relationship between God and man. Jesus himself gave us the mandate for relational theology when he affirmed the two greatest command-

ments: love God; love our brother. The Scriptures further
suggest that if we cannot love our brother whom we have
seen then we cannot love God whom we have not seen.

The Sermon on the Mount is a plea for new relationships
to God, our brothers and ourselves. We are enjoined repeatedly in the New Testament to love God with our whole
hearts—to love our neighbor *as we love ourselves;* to lay
down our lives for our friends; to love the world with food
for the hungry, water for the thirsty, clothes for the naked.
And by our love or lack of it in these relationships we are
judged.

There is a growing feeling that much of the "orthodox"
theology we have inherited from past decades is not really
biblical. Our problem seems to be that much of our previous
teaching has been received from great and trusted Christian
teachers whose lives and witness have been meaningful and
authentic. But anyone who has taken a course in logic is
aware of the fallaciousness of arguing *ad hominem*—in other
words, to discount someone's argument because of his questionable character or integrity. For example, if a known
thief rushed into a building shouting "fire," people would
tend to act on his word even though his character was not
reliable. A rogue or a charlatan can still be telling the truth.

Now the reverse is just as true. I have been guilty of as-
suming that any person of unquestioned faith and integrity
must at the same time be a custodian of truth. I no longer
accept that idea. Good and sincere people full of God's Holy
Spirit can be wrong and may unwittingly be teaching and
passing on error or even heresy. It is essential for each of us
to examine what we are being taught to see if it checks with
our own experience of life and ultimately with the Bible.

Relational theology as well needs to be submitted to this
double check. Perhaps many of the things we question don't

check with our experience. And as we examine the Bible, we may find that they are not biblical truths at all. As a young man and a new Christian, I remember hearing one of my spiritual heroes—a great preacher, author, and evangelist—state over and over again that social change could come about only by changing men's hearts; that you could not legislate morality. By changing men's hearts, laws would be passed which would eventually change society. Now, that sounded logical to me, and for a number of years I preached it. But later I began to examine that precept in the light of recent history. I realized that in spite of Christian preaching aimed at changing men's hearts, integration in the South first succeeded when the Army actually imposed change. White and black soldiers for the first time were forced to live together. I know of many hearts that were changed as a result of the integration instituted by the Army and later reinforced by the Supreme Court.

As threatening as it may seem to the fabric of our beliefs, even Paul, with his impeccable faith and credentials, accepted certain things we can't endorse today. Paul accepted slavery. Rather than urging slaves to overthrow their masters, he passed on rules of behavior for slaves and masters alike. Then too, Paul was convinced that Christ's second coming was imminent and that believers should not make any long-range plans. If even Paul at times suffered aberrations of belief, it seems to me we have a mandate to examine and question a good many present theological "truths" in the light of fresh understanding received from the Bible and from our own experience. Consequently, I want to do just that—examine the underlying basis for a working relational theology as it would apply to the Christian faith. This is not an attempt to cover the whole spectrum, but rather to indicate a new theological direction and emphasis.

The Personhood of God

Relational theology makes a distinction between God and the religion *about* God. For God and religion are by no means the same thing. The Bible seems to suggest that religion may even be the enemy of God. It was the religious people who crucified Jesus and who most incurred his wrath. To love God, in the biblical sense, is to emphasize the dimension of relationship as over against rules. Certainly there are guidelines for conduct and attitude—the Ten Commandments, the Beatitudes, and the great commandment that Jesus gave. But the Bible is not essentially a book of rules. It is a book about a living God who wants to enter into a relationship with his created beings. And this relationship is marked by love and forgiveness on God's part and honesty, openness and receptivity on ours.

In 1 Samuel 13, David is called a man after God's own heart. Now, David had broken the rules flagrantly. He was a liar, a murderer, an adulterer, and a cheat. But David could face up to his wrongs; he could repent and make restitution. The great fact of his life was the love and forgiveness of God. Relational theology simply emphasizes the central fact of all the Bible: man's relationship to God on his terms, a relationship between Forgiver and forgiven, between Lover and loved.

If God is seen primarily as judge and rule-giver, keeping those rules becomes all important. This inevitably leads to a necessity for justifying oneself at every point. If we stress rules rather than relationship, then it is important to prove that I am a hapless victim and that someone else is really responsible when I have broken the rules. That is the supreme cop-out.

At various times in my own life, I have found myself repeatedly confessing to God that I have been too busy for a

longer prayer time or for more regular Bible reading. One
day I realized how dishonest this was. No matter how busy
I was I found time to eat and sleep and bathe. When I could
finally level with God and say, "I'm not too busy. I guess I
really don't love you enough and don't want to spend more
time with you. That is my problem," a turning point came
in my relationship to God. God could forgive my self-
centeredness or my shallow, immature love. But pretending
that I couldn't spend more time with him because of the
busy schedule he had imposed upon me broke the relationship. In other words, I was blaming God because I wasn't
praying more. He had given me too much to do. In my new
relationship with him it is essential that I try to be absolutely honest. The miracle of that relationship is God's un-
conditional love for me as I am.

The Nature of Faith

What is faith in the context of relational theology? We
have a popular understanding of faith today which implies
that if you have enough faith you will not be sick and you
will not be in trouble. Rather, with enough faith you will be
healthy, wealthy, and "victorious"—always able to cope. It
seems to me this has more to do with magic than with real
faith.

Again, if we examine the lives of those people in the Bible
who lived by faith, we find that more often than not their
faith got them into trouble. What we remember most about
the story of Shadrack, Meshack and Abednigo is their de-
livery from the fiery furnace, but that is quite incidental.
It was their great faith in God which got them thrown into
the furnace in the first place. What we must also remember
is that many early Christian martyrs whose faith got them
thrown into the arena with the lions were never delivered.

Or listen to the Apostle Paul, who in 2 Corinthians 11:24–27 writes, "Five times I have received at the hands of the Jews the forty lashes less one. Three times I have been beaten with rods; once I was stoned. Three times I have been shipwrecked; a night and a day I have been adrift at sea; on frequent journeys, in danger from rivers, danger from robbers, danger from my own people, danger from Gentiles, danger in the city, danger in the wilderness, danger at sea, danger from false brethren; in toil and hardship, through many a sleepless night, in hunger and thirst, often without food, in cold and exposure" (RSV). Paul not only mentions physical dangers, he concludes that statement by saying, "And apart from other things, there is the daily pressure upon me of my anxiety for all the churches."

In some circles today the faithful brethren would hold prayer meetings for someone with problems like Paul's. They might even try to exorcise the demon by the laying on of hands. Because, for this group, the mark of faith is that one is somehow delivered from *all* the trials and tribulations of life. The biblical view, however, is that faith in Jesus Christ keeps getting us into trouble. Being saved by the grace of God in Jesus Christ means that we no longer have to play it safe. We are free to engage in the risky living Paul modeled.

A life without danger, without risk, without persecution, without cost, is not the life of authentic faith. Karl Wallenda and his family are perhaps the greatest high-wire acrobats in the world. In 1962 several members of the Wallenda troop fell from the wire and were killed while performing in Detroit. Just a few days later it was announced that those who survived would be back on the high wire repeating their famous act. When a reporter questioned Karl Wallenda, the senior member of the troop, about the decision, he said, "To be on the wire is life. All else is waiting."

For me, that statement seems to capture what it means to live by faith. Your faith puts you where there is danger, where you might be misunderstood, where you may suffer at the hands of friends and enemies alike.

The Test of Orthodoxy

How do we measure what and who is authentic? What are the standards by which we proclaim a believer true, genuine?

One of my own early spiritual heroes taught me that "unless one is winning [converts], one is sinning." And, conversely, that "when one is sinning, one cannot be winning." In other words, I would be leading people to Christ regularly and frequently if I were truly in the will of God. I still find myself at times straining in relationships to "win someone." It is hard to overcome those deep-rooted feelings that "winning" marks my own authenticity as a Christian.

There are various other tests of authenticity or orthodoxy, depending upon the group you're in. For some it is the number of Bible verses memorized. Perhaps the most common test is the degree to which one can abstain from doing "evil," however "evil" is defined by that particular group. In the past, one of the tests was "keeping the Sabbath." This might mean merely abstaining from worldly pleasure on that day or it could entail observing the Sabbath on Saturday instead of Sunday. There are still many groups who equate orthodoxy with a "no frills" style of life. They are the "plain folk" who wear no makeup and no fancy clothes. Another test of orthodoxy has to do with the use of money. Tithing is expected and giving beyond the tithe is encouraged. And in the early Protestant tradition orthodoxy was related to the glorifying of hard work, the saving of money and the avoidance of frivolous spending. In other traditions the ultimate is to renounce all salaries and simply "live by faith." For still others the test of orthodoxy is the degree and efficacy of prayer as defined by that group. It is measured by the number of hours spent faithfully at prayer each day, or perhaps by the kind of prayer and whether or not it includes speaking and praying in tongues. And there are those who measure orthodoxy by the proportion of prayers answered, especially prayers for physical, spiritual, or mental healing.

Certainly all of the above practices have some basis in Scripture. But to make any of them the ultimate test of orthodoxy, explicitly or implicitly, is not scriptural. In relational theology we say emphatically that the quality and scope of relationships and the ability and willingness to relate are marks of orthodoxy rather than doctrine, ethical performance or spiritual heroism.

This concept, it seems to me, is in direct opposition to the notion that orthodoxy can be measured by one's biblical knowledge or theological certainty, one's lack of vices or one's good works, with soul-winning perhaps the ultimate good work. The Bible does not verify these concepts at all. Rather it speaks about relating to God in love, in trust, and in honesty; about relating in love to our neighbor. The Bible speaks about loving the world for which Christ died by feeding the hungry and caring for the sick and passing out cups of cold water to the thirsty—thereby proving one's love for Christ. The second chapter of Acts indicates that when believers are about this primary purpose, converts are added automatically.

But the fact that one's orthodoxy is measured by these relationships does not eliminate the need for sound doctrine, for noble ethics, and for acts of genuine heroism. All of these are important. But relational theology suggests that the primary biblical injunction is to relate in love to God, to self, and to others as the ultimate and authenticating mark of life in Christ. 1 Corinthians 13:1-3 is a singular proof-text for this view: "If I speak in the tongues of men and of angels, but have not love, I am a noisy gong or a clanging cymbal. And if I have prophetic powers, and understand all mysteries and all knowledge, and if I have all faith so as to remove mountains, but have not love, I am nothing. If I give away all I have, and if I deliver my body to be burned, but have not love, I gain nothing" (RSV). These verses seem to affirm that sound doctrine, ethical behavior, and genuine self-sacrifice are all good, but the mark of authentic orthodoxy is the relationship of love.

A Definition of the "New Creation"

The Bible says that if anyone be in Christ he is a "new creation." What does that mean? For years I have assumed that to be a new creation meant that I would be Christlike. I would be someone better, kinder, more loving, more generous and more concerned than a non-Christian. It was always embarrassing to me when I was asked questions about some great humanitarian who was not a Christian—questions like: "Do you think he/she needs to become a Christian? Look at all they are doing for others—how generous and kind they are!" I was secretly chagrined that God was using so many "good" people who were not yet Christians to minister to the world's needs.

Relational theology in no way equates the "new creation" with some kind of exemplary life. We are coming to understand that the new creation is not necessarily a better person than the non-Christian. This new creation may not be "victorious" in the commonly accepted sense. He may not be a wiser person than those around him. He is not some miracle-worker or a spiritual Mister Clean who prays every-

body well. The definition of the new creation basic to relational theology is first of all someone living a life-style based
on a new kind of relationship with God and man. Further,
that life-style embodies a vulnerable position, adopted by
conscious choice. Vulnerability is not a virtue if we are so
frightened, insecure, and full of self-hate that we are sub-
missive in every relationship. Christ's Spirit living in us
should be a source of tremendous affirmation about our own
worth and abilities. And from that new position of strength
we can choose to be vulnerable and to be a servant. This
vulnerability includes being honest about failures, sins, and
needs. It may mean undertaking risky projects that will in-
vite attack. It can also mean giving up earned places of
privilege and position or lending money with slight chance
of ever seeing it again. And it may mean sharing dreams
even though you are misunderstood. This new creation
personifies a lack of defensiveness that can open the doors
to all kinds of creative relationships.

Also, the new creation in Christ is someone who can affirm others in the same way that Christ has affirmed us. The
Bible tells us Christ died for us while we were yet unworthy.
The new creation, while not necessarily wiser, better, or
kinder than his neighbors, is able to affirm the worth of
others while it is still hidden. An excellent example of this
is found in the New Testament story of Barnabas, who is
called the son of encouragement because his presence gave
those around him a sense of their own worth. By contrast,
most of us are naturally and instinctively defensive in our
relationships. We are guilty of being either openly critical
or of deliberately withholding this kind of affirmation. To
call forth the best in another person and to allow relationships through personal vulnerability requires a radical
change, in fact, a "new creation."

The Place of Change

How strange it is that a great many Christians, past and present, have been identified with reactionary movements and an unwillingness to change. We are locked in with the familiar and feel somehow that *old* music is better than new, that *old* forms are better than new, that *old* values are superior to the new. A Gothic church building is not necessarily superior to a contemporary church in the round. A Bach chorale is not inherently more worshipful in every situation than contemporary music, whatever comparisons you may wish to make about the two musically. To live is to change. I like the way Mildred Newman and Bernard Berkowitz express it in *How To Be Your Own Best Friend:* "If we all just kept on doing what we've done up to now, people would never change, and people are changing all the time. That's what growth is: doing things you've never done before, sometimes things you once didn't even dream you could."

Relational theology stresses that God, who is unchanging in his personhood and goals, is always changing in his strategy. God is a God of change in both the Old and the New Testament. Three thousand years ago he said to his people, "Remember not the former things, nor consider the things of old. Behold, I am doing a new thing; . . . do you not perceive it?" (Isa. 43:18, RSV). In other words, the old things are not necessarily better. If God is in the business of perfecting his people, then change must be in order.

Change is the means by which God can give something new to his people. If we oppose change, we are resisting the very act by which God can perfect us and sanctify us and help us. And if we believe that the three great verities in life are faith, hope, and love, then we must deal with the fact that hope is an attitude about a future state which can only be ushered in by change. Perhaps this is one of the most difficult ideas to understand and accept and live with emotionally. But Christians need to be excited by change, expectant about it. Indeed, Christians should feel at home in change, for God is the initiator of much change.

Defining Salvation

In the context of relational theology, salvation is always incomplete. Now, we believe we are saved by the sacrifice of Jesus Christ on Calvary's cross in the great drama of redemption and that nothing we can do adds to that starting point. But, salvation as man experiences it is something much vaster than the initial conversion event, and it is never complete in this world.

The whole idea of salvation comes from the Latin word *salus,* which means health or wholeness. Modern medicine is being revolutionized right now because of the new awareness that health is more than the absence of illness— it is the presence of positive factors. So in the spiritual realm, wholeness means more than having one's sin dealt with. In Jesus Christ and his love and sacrifice on the cross, God dealt with our sins. But having claimed that forgiveness, there is much that we must do to choose life.

Paul says in Philippians 2:12–13, ". . . Work out your own salvation with fear and trembling; for God is at work in you, both to will and to work for his good pleasure" (RSV). We are saved by Christ from our sins, but the adding to our lives of those positive ingredients that God wants us to have is the ongoing process of salvation. We come together to worship, to study, to break bread, and to have fellowship, accepting the fact that we are not complete. God is working in us and we must work with him to discover all that we are meant to be as his people.

The writers of the New Testament are certainly aware of this. Peter writes in 2 Peter 1:5-9 that it is certainly possible to have a saving faith, but he would like to see believers add goodness to that faith. Beyond faith and goodness he wants them to add knowledge. And the goal beyond faith and goodness and knowledge is self-control. Then the list goes on to include endurance and godliness and brotherly love and love. He adds, "These are the qualities you need, and if you have them in abundance they will make you active and effective in your knowledge of our Lord Jesus Christ. But whoever does not have them is so short-sighted that he cannot see, and has forgotten that his past sins have been washed away" (TEV).

Understanding Sanctification

If we are always incomplete, is the idea of sanctification alien to the concept of relational theology? How do we define sanctification in terms of relational theology? Being sanctified does not mean that we are sinners emeritus, that we once sinned, but don't any more. There are Christians who imply this and even teach it. Yet in 1 John where we are told to walk in the light, it reads, "If we say we have no sin, we deceive ourselves, and the truth is not in us. If we confess our sins, he is faithful and just, and will forgive our sins and cleanse us from all unrighteousness. If we say we have not sinned, we make him a liar, and his word is not in us" (1 John 1:8-10, RSV). Then John continues, "My little children, I am writing this to you so that you may not sin; but if anyone does sin, we have an advocate with the Father, Jesus Christ the righteous" (1 John 2:1, RSV).

I believe sanctification describes a state where we are so secure in our experience with God's love and forgiveness that we are free to walk in the light, exposing our sins, failings, and shortcomings. This is freedom! Again, if we go back to the fact that we are talking about a relationship to God rather than keeping rules, then sanctification does not depend on having kept the rules. Sanctification is instead synonymous with a kind of defenselessness where we can enjoy the fact that God loves us and accepts us and continues to forgive us. It is emotionally and intellectually standing firmly on the great Eternal Truth.

This is a difficult way to live. I am a naturally defensive person. I would like to believe that because I am Christ's man, filled with his Spirit and sanctified, I don't sin in the same old way. But to be sanctified means taking my own failings much less seriously because God has taken them so very seriously.

Recently we moved to Sanibel, a delightful community situated on an island in the Gulf of Mexico just off the coast at Fort Myers. This means that we're going through the trauma of establishing new relationships. Not long after our move I needed desperately to see a dentist. I found one listed in the yellow pages of the telephone book who agreed to see me early the next day. The next morning I started out across the causeway to the mainland, and as luck would have it the drawbridge was up, so I was seven minutes late for my appointment. Just as I was about to blame my lateness on the open drawbridge, I realized that an excuse wouldn't help either of us. The dentist's justifiable anger at having to wait would have no place to land, and he would probably transfer his feelings to other patients the rest of the day. So, I decided to tell the truth! "I'm sorry I'm late, doctor. I guess I'm just incompetent to handle my life at times. Please forgive me." *

---

* This came from a suggestion made by Dr. William Glasser at a workshop.

After a momentary expression of amazement, his face cracked into a broad smile, and he assured me it was okay and he understood. I wish I could feel this kind of freedom more often. Perhaps here is a clue to what sanctification is all about—being defenseless before our peers, especially when we are wrong. I identify so often with the story of Uzzah in the Old Testament. The Israelites were moving the ark in an oxcart and, since they were told that God dwelt in the ark, no man was ever to touch it. But Uzzah was a man who, when he saw the ark of God wobbling, reached out to prop it up and promptly died. There is such a strong need in me to help God, to prop up his reputation by my impeccable conduct, and to be a know-it-all Christian who is never off base. But I'm sure God can even sing his song through me when I am free to be the failing, sinning, stumbling self who knows he is loved and who can love himself and even the people he has failed.

A Relationship with the World

One particular brand of Christian thought implies the "world" is an evil place, a place into which Christians go after much prayer and then only to perform some act of service. But relational theology sees the world as the arena for God's actions. It is the world for which Christ died. I just can't accept a distinction between "secular" or "sacred." For me, at least, that is phony.

The church is not a better place than the world nor is the world a worse place than the church. Christ died for both. The church is simply the place where the lordship of Christ is acknowledged and where we have chosen to try to be obedient to him. We have given him the right to set the agenda and focus the goals for our life. We are under new management and have new priorities. From the church we go into the world to be a part of God's creative will and purpose. In a very real sense every Christian needs the world. It ministers to us. We meet God there in the sick, the poor, the hungry, and the prisoner, just as he said we would. If we ignore our brother in the world, we are ignoring God (Matt. 25:45). God is in the world, and we discover our own souls as we lay down our lives for our brothers "out there."

The Question of Sin

In relational theology we believe that we are separated from God only by our refusal to accept his love and forgiveness. To me, this means that we sin either by our pretense of innocence or because of our inability to believe that God can deal with our particular sin. Both Peter and Judas sinned against the Lord. Both were ashamed and guilty. Peter, who had denied him, waited heartbroken until the risen Christ returned to tell him he was loved and commissioned him to build his kingdom. Judas, on the other hand, believing his sin was unforgivable, hanged himself. To believe that God can forgive sins in Jesus Christ but not "my particular sin" reflects the kind of egocentrism which is in itself the very heart of sin.

God's attitude toward sin is revealed in Genesis in his relationship with Adam. Though Adam had sinned, deliberately and knowingly, God still called out to Adam in the Garden. God hadn't withdrawn in shock and horror; it was Adam who was hiding. In response to his question, Adam tells God he hid out of fear, but his next words are more an excuse than a confession: "The woman you gave me for a companion, she gave me fruit from the tree and I ate it" (Gen. 3:12, NEB). He blames both God and his wife for his predicament. What a familiar pattern!

Two other contrasting examples are Aaron, Moses' brother-in-law, and King David. Perhaps no one ever sinned more both quantitatively and qualitatively (and I might add diversely) than King David. But when conviction came, he could take the blame, make restitution where possible, and claim forgiveness. Not only did he claim forgiveness, he celebrated publicly the incredible fact that he was forgiven by God. Aaron, on the other hand, when he is discovered leading the Israelites in worship of a golden calf which he has built while Moses was away, said in effect, "It's not my fault. We simply put all our jewelry into this fire and out came this golden calf. I'm innocent." Aaron was probably less guilty than David in terms of degree of sin, but he pretended he was innocent.

Perhaps our chief sin is the fact that we pretend we have not sinned. This makes God redundant, Jesus Christ unnecessary, and Calvary foolishness. We undo the higher groundwork on which a relationship to God can be maintained. Whenever I am describing a disagreement or confrontation with someone, I find myself using words like, "All I said was . . ." I am caught in the old trap of asserting my innocence. It's difficult to be in a relationship of love with someone who is never wrong, isn't it?

As I conduct workshops for different groups around the country, I often have them do this interesting exercise: "Think of the most difficult relationship you are in right now and describe this to your workshop partner without using a single bit of history—no details of how the relationship got this way." Many people are frustrated in this exercise because the only way they can describe an unfulfilling relationship is to provide a history which makes *them* the innocent party. Too often we see our difficulties in terms of our own innocence. But when I stop seeing myself as a victim and realize that I am in a relationship of my own choosing then I can choose to change the relationship.

The Guidance of the Holy Spirit

Essential to relational theology is the belief that God's
Holy Spirit is constantly speaking to his children, trying to
guide us in the major decisions as well as the small ones.
But there is always the danger that *getting* guidance may
become more important than a relationship with the Giver
of the guidance. People who believe that simply because
they have prayed and listened and, consequently, are doing
God's will in a given situation are in trouble if this becomes
the foundation for their faith. Our faith rests on the fact
that we are loved by God the Father and Creator; we are
redeemed by the love and sacrifice of Jesus Christ the Lord;
and his Holy Spirit lives his life within us when we allow
him to. That is better than just being "guided."

Fundamental to a relational theology is the conviction that
a Christian can never be positive that he is guided. If he were
positive, then he would not need "the Guider," and there
would be no necessity for faith to trust the Guider. Faith
and commitment in the relationship can survive even what
may prove to be mistaken guidance. The Book of Acts reports that the early Christians made a great many mistakes
even though they prayed and listened to the Spirit. But they
were God's people and were not afraid to fail. There was
willingness to risk, and, inevitably, they sometimes were
wrong about God's leading. But their certainty was in their
relationship to a Lord who was with them, who loved them,
and who would not desert them even when they misunderstood his will.

Today, our certainty does not depend upon our faithful-
ness or goodness or our ability to receive guidance from God
or upon whether we are used by his Holy Spirit to help
others. Rather, our certainty is based on our Lord's word
that he will never leave us nor forsake us. Our certainty is

based on what *he* has said and on what *he* has done. Therefore, even if I am not always certain that what I am about to
do is God's will simply because I have prayed and believe I
have listened to him, I am not afraid—even if I may be
wrong. I hope that what I do in a given situation is God's
will, and I pray that it is. But if I am truly in Christ and
discover that I have been wrong, I am free to say, "I sure
blew that one." At that moment God loves me no less than
he did when I was in the very center of his will.

For years I kept a quiet time in the morning. I think I was
secretly hoping that my time with God would give me an
edge on everyone else for the rest of the day. I believed that
if God could really transmit his ideas to me, then I would
move through life one notch above those about me. Following my early morning vigil, I arrived at the breakfast table
absolutely sure I had God's word for the day, and I was eager
to be God's best for my wife and children. So often, though,
I was disillusioned because I would be the first one to lose his
temper and the last to love and forgive. I would misunder-
stand something someone said and break the spirit of love
in the family. Not until years later did I realize that God
was trying to tell me our quiet time together was for reas-
surance that I *was loved,* that I *am loved,* that I *will be
loved*—that I am eternally "home free" and even a bad performance on my part will not change that.

In John Osborne's popular play *Luther,* Luther is visited
by Staupitz, an old friend and teacher from the early mon-
astery days. Many years have passed, the Reformation is a
fact, and Staupitz has remained loyal to Rome. In this very
moving scene where these two old friends meet, Staupitz
asks Luther why he needed an extra day to think over his
reply to the two vital questions that were put to him at the
Diet of Worms. After all, Martin had told him ahead of time
what his answer would be.

Luther confesses to his friend that when the chips were down he really wasn't certain and he needed some time to listen to God's voice. Staupitz then asks if he was certain after that day of listening. Luther replies that he listened for God's voice but all that he could hear was his own. Staupitz then asks if he was certain after that. Finally, after a long pause, Luther says, "No."

For me, this exemplifies the miraculous expression of authentic faith. One acts on what he feels is God's guidance, but ultimately is not completely certain. The only thing we can be sure of is that we are loved and are forgiven, and this transcends even the experience of God's guidance.

Relational Theology and Eschatology

In spite of the popular notion that pervades certain segments of Christian thought, I believe that these days may very well be the first rather than the last days. In some sense we may be in a pre-Christian rather than a post-Christian era.

The Bible tells us clearly that no one knows when the last days will be. And the Bible even warns us to be suspicious of people who claim to know when the last days will be. It goes so far as to call some of these people false prophets (see Matt. 24:23-28). I get the feeling here that we are not to be preoccupied with eschatology, not to worry about when the last days will be. All things are in God's hands, and he will take care of them in good time. Our business is to be about his business. Christ has come in his Spirit and is here now calling us to obedience, to evangelization of the world, and to ministry.

We must bear in mind that for centuries many people of faith have prophesied with absolute sincerity that the last days were imminent; obviously they've been wrong so far.

Even the Apostle Paul seems to have labored under some misconceptions.

But for me, at least, the future is in God's hands, and I don't feel impelled to match up isolated Scripture portions in an attempt to blueprint his will for me or the world. I guess the most important thing is my own attitude about the time ahead of me. In reading the words of the Apostle Paul, I find it interesting that as time goes on he dwells less upon the last days and significantly more on how to live in this life. When he is writing as a new Christian, he is preoccupied with the last days. But his latter writings seem to take into account the fact that Christ's coming may be further into the future.

When will the Lord come again? Only he knows. But it seems to me that the important thing, whether I have six days, six months, one year, or the rest of a long lifetime, is the quality of my life, my enthusiasm for his kingdom, my commitment to all people in his name, and my overall sense of hope. I guess, since no one knows the times or the seasons, I would rather live my life as an architect of God's new order even for a short time than to spend a long life being a rear-guard action for the people of God.

The Christian's Stance

An interesting phenomenon has emerged with regard to those of us involved in relational theology. Some Christian conservatives think of us as dangerously liberal. On the other hand, many liberals have regarded us as hopelessly conservative. Probably there is a good reason for both suspicions, and perhaps this confusing image is our most distinctive mark.

Until recently the Christian church had been divided into two main groups. The first group consisted of the doctrinal

conservatives of many shades who were also politically conservative. Then, there were the theological liberals who were
also politically liberal. But beginning in the early 1960s, a
growing number of us in the church found ourselves increasingly uncomfortable in either camp. The social and political liberal who experienced a genuine personal conversion
to Jesus Christ felt uncomfortable in conservative churches
because of their reactionary stance to change and their lack
of involvement in the current social scene. On the other
hand, many conservative-minded Christians began to find
God in new ways through involvement in the anti-war and
social liberation movements of the '60s. But, unfortunately,
the theologically liberal churches failed in the proclamation
of a gospel centering in the person of Jesus Christ as Lord
and Savior. The results are now history. But a third
force began to emerge which is not a *via media* between the
old liberals and conservatives. Rather, a new breed of people
are discovering a position which is unashamedly conservative in theology and liberal in its view of man.

Perhaps this dichotomy is as old as the faith. In the Old
Testament the year of Jubilee was established by God to
insure "liberal" policies by the Israelites every fifty years.
He did not trust his "chosen people" to treat their brothers
with mercy and compassion. At fifty-year intervals all slaves
were freed, all debts cancelled and all land returned to its
owners. Jesus began his own earthly ministry by reminding
his listeners of these prophetic words: "The Spirit of the
Lord is upon me, because he has anointed me to preach good
news to the poor. He has sent me to proclaim release to the
captives and recovering of sight to the blind, to set at liberty those who are oppressed, and to proclaim the acceptable
year of the Lord." He then ended his remarks with these
words: "Today this scripture has been fulfilled in your hearing" (Luke 4:18–19, 21, RSV).

Surely a proclamation of liberal and humanitarian policies by Jesus himself dictates a liberal and humanitarian position for the authentic people of God. Christ emerges as the great humanist in the true sense of the word, while calling people to genuine piety and devotion to him as their Lord and Savior. From this, it seems to me that relational theology establishes what God always had in mind for his people—personal piety, coupled with a view of man's needs and his potential which can only be characterized as humanitarian.

Conclusion

These are a few of the concepts that have come to me about the Christian life and its theological overtones. Relational theology means for me that all of the usual theological questions—sin, faith, guidance, sanctification, the personhood of God—are seen in the relational dimension and are viewed in terms of a primary relationship with God, ourselves, our brothers, and the world.

Above all, relational theology insists that the Good News is beyond all theology—relational or otherwise. It is based on the belief that God has entered into a relationship with us of unbreakable love and all-encompassing forgiveness which is sealed by the life, sacrifice, death, and resurrection of Jesus Christ, his Son.

7. RESOURCES FOR THE REVOLUTION

"PREACHER, don't waste your time on her. She's a lost ball in the high weeds!" One of our town's leading psychiatrists was briefing me on the phone about a patient who was to begin counseling with me. I was calling to get her case history.

It all began when this young woman phoned. She had found my name in the yellow pages under "Clergy," and was calling me as a last resort. For three years she had been under the care of the finest psychiatrist in our area and had spent much time in some of the most expensive private sanitariums in our state. Currently she had her own apartment with a live-in psychiatric nurse and was seeing her psychiatrist three times a week. She was on a number of drugs and seemed to be getting no better. Her psychiatrist gave her no hope for a return to her normal life, which included a responsible job in a specialized educational program.

When I agreed to see her, she suggested I call her psychiatrist for the background information on her case. He told me she had been victimized in unspeakable ways by her family and had every right to be seriously ill and unable to function. In spite of his "lost ball" reaction, I decided to take her on.

With her nurse in attendance, she came to my office three times a week. During those next months I tried every spiritual and psychiatric resource I knew, including prayer, the laying on of hands, the healing of memories, confession and absolution in the name of Jesus. She did not respond. I had been counseling her for nearly a year when I received a call to another church. We talked over the fact that I could no longer see her. What did she want to do? She still had hope that God could help her, though she refused to start all over again with another clergyman. As an alternative, I suggested she join one of our church's small groups which were meeting for prayer, Bible study, and the sharing of life together. They met weekly in homes around the city. Reluctantly, she decided to join one that very week, but only if I agreed to tell them nothing about her history.

They took her in, as I knew they would, and asked no questions. For six weeks she said nothing more than hello and good-by. But three months after she joined that group, she fired her live-in nurse. In another three months she stopped taking her pills. Three months after that she was dismissed by her psychiatrist. And three months later (one year after joining the group) she was back at her very specialized job in education. No one in the group was aware of having done anything unusual, but they knew they had witnessed a miracle. This girl's astonishing experience contradicted everything I had come to expect as a professional. That was my first awareness of what I have since come to call the resource revolution.

God first began to reach me on this through the experience with that young woman. But an increasing number of such experiences in the years since then have convinced me that God has made unlimited resources available for helping people through the ordinary, untrained nonprofessional. In the language of the church, I believe he has in fact called every believer to be a priest of love and healing to others.

In the physical world, we are just coming to an appreciation of the natural resources God has made available to us. In all likelihood, atomic or solar power will replace gas, coal, oil, or wood as a source of fuel and energy. I am told that enough energy from the sun falls on Lake Erie in a single day to provide the United States with all her energy needs for an entire year. It is ironic that for years we scoured the world looking for cheap resources of coal and oil while all around us was an infinite supply of natural resources, such as sunshine or splittable atoms.

In the relational dimension, I believe God, through ordinary people, has made natural resources available for help and healing. Further, it seems to me that we are in the *kairos* (the biblical Greek word for the fullness of time or right moment) for the unleashing of these natural resources. Here are some thoughts on why this might be so.

The Need for More Personalized Care

One of the most hopeful things taking place in the people-serving vocations today is the awareness that health cannot be mass-produced, that in the medical field effective diagnosis and treatment must be on a one-to-one basis. For education to have its maximal impact there must be a one-to-one relationship between the student and the teacher. In penology it is becoming increasingly evident that only the programs in which individuals voluntarily spend time with prisoners on a one-to-one basis are effective. Even churches which specialize in the cure of souls are aware of the need of a one-to-one approach in helping people to grow and find their full potential. The power of the one to one is being realized in all the people-helping fields.

There are simply not enough professionals available presently in the fields of education, medicine, psychiatry, religion, or social work to meet these growing needs if help is to become more personalized. The area of mental health alone provides one dramatic example. The World Health Organization says that no country has enough staff to recognize and deal with more than a few of those needing mental care. (Some European countries have twelve psychiatrists per hundred thousand population, some have one per hundred thousand, while most developing countries have only one per several million people.)

The parallel between the diminishing supply of needed professionals and the diminishing oil supply for the world's energy needs is striking. However we hoard our fossil fuel resources, eventually the supply will run out. Just as alternative measures must be found for energy, new resources must be found in all the helping professions.

As the demand increases for more person-to-person care in the major helping fields, we realize the built-in limitations of our present approach. We have an arithmetic supply and a geometric need. We have neither the schools and faculties available to train enough professionals to meet this fast growing need nor the money required to do so. Even if we could train enough professionals in every field, the cost of their services in many instances would be prohibitive.

Finding a New Resource

Obviously, the only solution is to tap and train the vast alternative resources. Most of the helping professions already make extensive use of volunteers and nonprofessionals. This is not new. What is new in our time is the growing awareness that in some cases the paraprofessional or nonprofessional is better able to do the job than the professional. The idea must be abandoned that we are using amateurs or paraprofessionals because "the real thing" is not available. Rather, from studies made in many fields, there is a weight of evidence that the professionals have been largely ineffective.

For example, there are growing suspicions about the effectiveness of both psychiatry and psychotherapy. As long ago as June 1962, the now-defunct *New York Herald Tribune* ran a feature article by Earl Ubell, its science editor, stating that exhaustive tests made up to that time indicated that none of the major schools of psychotherapy have had any measurable results. For example, he reported on a test made on seventy-five psychoneurotics in San Francisco. Half of the group were treated with psychotherapy; the others received no treatment at all. The test concluded that over the prescribed period the treated patients showed no changes not also apparent in the untreated group.

The same article reported on a study made by Dr. Eugene Levitt, a psychologist then at the Illinois Institute for Juvenile Research, and two associates. Of 469 emotionally disturbed children, 327 were treated with psychotherapy, while another 142 received no treatment. Observing the group five years later, Dr. Levitt said, "There is no difference at follow-up between the adjustments made by the treated and untreated child patients." Later Dr. Levitt surveyed 37 investigations involving 8,000 patients given psychotherapy at different clinics. Again, he found no differences between the treated and untreated groups. When I read that startling article back in 1962, I expected subsequent protestations and denials from the professionals, and even some lawsuits, but none came. As a matter of fact, since that time an avalanche of similar tests has substantiated what Ubell reported so prophetically more than a decade ago.*

----

* Some of the best-known and most recent tests concerning this hypothesis are listed in the notes in the back of Thomas Oden's *Game Free* (New York: Harper & Row, 1974).

Now if these studies are accurate, then nonprofessionally trained persons can begin to do much counseling that only professionals have done up until now. Obviously, the reservoir for this kind of natural resource is practically unlimited. Imagine the vast resources among senior citizens who have a lifetime of experience to share. But even folk in the middle years, faced as they are with extended leisure and a shrinking work week, offer a growing potential as every person becomes a resource for his neighbor.

It is no longer shocking that an untrained small group can sometimes work with a "lost ball in the high weeds" and obtain more results than the professionals. In general this has been true in helping alcoholics. With the birth of Alcoholics Anonymous in 1935, a new approach to therapy emerged using *only* untrained nonprofessionals. Previously, alcoholism had for the most part baffled both medicine and psychiatry. The incidence of cure or remission was pathetically small. In the 1940s, I talked with a number of doctors and psychiatrists who refused to accept alcoholic patients because they considered them hopeless. Since Alcoholics Anonymous began, hundreds of thousands of people have stopped drinking with the help and support of nonprofessionals who are also alcoholics.

From that beginning, a number of similar helping fellowships emerged: Synanon, Teen Challenge, Gamblers Anonymous, and a variety of weight-reduction programs. The resource revolution has begun and will flourish, I believe, because we are living with the successful results achieved by the untrained layman in areas where the professional seems generally to have been less than effective. This demonstration of the power of ordinary people to help others is forcing leaders from the helping professions to reevaluate the future of professional therapy in all fields.

Overcoming Our Inferiority as Nonprofessionals

What are those factors that seem to bring healing or help to persons with problems? I think it is important in responding to this question to recognize that even though much therapy and counseling may be proven ineffective, there are singularly effective persons, both amateur and professional, who have the ability to help other people. For example, why was my "lost ball in the high weeds" helped so powerfully by that untrained, nonprofessional small group?

First, the people in the group dared to get involved. We often refrain from involvement with a person in trouble because of a culturally induced sense of inferiority. We instinctively think, "I just don't know enough to help." A nonprofessional must rid himself of the feeling that healing and help come only from some therapeutic technique or some complicated theory of personality.

One of the most articulate spokesmen for this common-sense approach is psychiatrist William Glasser. Here are six areas where he takes issue with conventional psychiatry.*

1. Conventional psychiatry believes firmly that mental illness is a reality; sufferers can be meaningfully classified and attempts should be made to treat them according to the diagnostic classification.

Glasser believes there is no such thing as mental illness and that people are responsible for their behavior.

2. Conventional psychiatry holds that an essential part of treatment is probing into the patient's past life, searching for the psychological roots of the problem. Once the patient clearly understands these roots he can use his understanding

---

* These points are taken from his book *Reality Therapy* (New York: Harper & Row, 1965).

to change his attitude toward life. From this change in attitude he can develop more effective patterns of living to solve his psychological difficulties.

Glasser avoids getting involved with a patient's history. He works in the present and toward the future because the patient cannot change what has happened to him. Glasser does not accept the dictum that the patient is limited by the past.

3. Conventional psychiatry maintains that the patient must transfer to the therapist his attitudes toward the important people in his past life, people with whom his problems began. Using this kind of transference, the therapist helps the patient relive past difficulties and then points out that the same inadequate behavior is being repeated with the therapist. Through the therapist's interpretation of the transference behavior the patient gains insight into the past. The insight allows him to give up his old attitudes and to relate to people in a healthier way.

Glasser insists on relating to his patients as himself, not as the transference figure.

4. Conventional psychiatry even in superficial counseling emphasizes that, to change, the patient must gain insight into his unconscious mind. Unconscious mental conflicts are considered more important than conscious problems. The patient is made aware of these unconscious conflicts through free association, interpretation of transference and of dreams, and through educated psychiatric guessing.

Glasser is not interested in unconscious conflicts or the reasons for them. The patient, he says, must not be allowed to excuse his behavior on the basis of unconscious motivations.

5. Conventional psychiatry scrupulously avoids the problem of morality; that is, making any judgments on the patient's behavior. Deviant behavior is the product of mental

illness and the patient isn't morally responsible because he
is unable to behave differently. Once the illness is cured
through the procedures described in points 2, 3, and 4, the
patient will be able to behave according to society's rules.

Glasser emphasizes moral behavior. He faces the issue of
right and wrong with his patients, convinced this solidifies
the involvement.

6. Promoting better behavior is not an important part of
conventional psychiatric therapy, which holds that behavior
will improve once the historical and unconscious sources of
problems are understood.

Glasser says the proper involvement will not be maintained unless the patient is helped to find more satisfactory
patterns of behavior, and he suggests to patients better ways
of fulfilling their needs.

Glasser's point of view, which represents those of a great
many innovative therapists in the field, is a Magna Carta
for people involved in lay counseling. First he punctures
some of the myths which have hampered the ordinary person from feeling adequate in dealing with someone else's
problems. Then, if Glasser is correct, anyone with average
ability and intellect and sensitivity can risk becoming involved with a fellow human who is struggling with a personal problem.

The Therapeutic Relationship

The second important factor in a helpful and healing relationship has to do with the quality of relationship between
the counselor and the counselee. This insight is not exactly
new. In graduate school in 1955 I did a major paper on the
work of F. E. Fiedler, who in the late 1940s researched the
effectiveness of various schools of psychology and psychia-

try. His studies support the hypothesis now held by a growing number of leaders in the field of therapy that the
therapist's attitude toward his patient, not his theory or
technique makes counseling therapeutic. Hence, it would
seem that the therapeutic element in all counseling is the
counseling relationship itself and the key to an effective
relationship is the proper attitude on the part of the counselor. And studies prove that the attitudes which produced
therapeutic relationships were nontransferable in the classroom, so we are talking about something beyond the academic.

Apparently some counselors have innate attitudes and
qualities which enable healing in the life of another person.
It is not difficult to make the transition, then, to the fact
that lay people with these same innate gifts can so cultivate
them that they can effectively help other people.

I remember hearing Carl Rogers say that if a person has
this ability to "relate," he can be trained to be a counselor
in a very short time. Without this natural ability, no amount
of training will make him effective. This from the father of
nondirective counseling!

Recently I talked to Dr. Paul Tournier, one of the best-
known counselors and therapists of our time. When I asked
him how he counsels people, he said, "I am very embarrassed by all these people who come to see me. I don't know
how to help people. I don't do anything at all. What is important is that people try to find their way and that I try to
understand and support them, to welcome them. What is
important is that people find me a true friend, someone in
whom they confide everything. What a privilege to find
someone in whom you can confide without fear of being
judged."

Dr. Tournier is not describing a professional relationship
but one of love and trust and empathy. This kind of relation-

ship is open to anyone willing to be a friend and to pay the price of friendship. Dr. Tournier certainly seems to validate the notion that we do not need long professional training to be effective resource people for others.

This quality of relationship is also being taken seriously in teacher training, where currently there is great discouragement with "professionalism." Dr. Arthur Combs, head of the Department of Education at the University of Florida in Gainesville, says that there is no right or good method for either teaching or training teachers. The key in education, according to Combs, is the spontaneous and instantaneous response to a person. In other words, self is the essential instrument in teaching. The teacher, through spontaneity and instantaneous response, uses his or her life as an enabling process to help another learn.

Dr. Morrell Klute, head of the Department of Education at Wayne State University in Detroit, Michigan, believes that no one ever teaches another human being. Rather, each individual teaches himself. He also feels that the whole idea of training one person to teach a subject to another is fallacious. Klute and Combs are articulate spokesmen for this revolutionary approach to teaching. They are wary of teacher training in the usual sense because so many people with no innate ability to call forth learning from another are given credentials. These two educators are laying the groundwork for the professionally untrained but naturally gifted to act as enablers of others.

Recruiting and Training Resources in the Church

Since its beginning, the Christian church has been in the forefront in the use of the untrained paraprofessional as a resource person. The New Testament tells us that every believer is a priest. Certainly the people of God could be pro-

viding a resource in any number of areas. A survey by the
American Medical Association revealed that doctors felt over
90 percent of the patients they saw each day actually had
emotional or personal problems rather than medical ones.
Unable to give an hour each to twenty-five different patients,
they are forced instead to prescribe tranquilizers.

How can we implement the recruiting and training of
paraprofessionals to begin to meet this great need? That is
an exciting and pregnant challenge for both the church and
medicine today.

The hotlines and help lines, mostly church-related telephone ministries, are a beginning. The following article from
our local Florida paper, the *Fort Myers News Press*, matter-
of-factly reports on one such local ministry.

> Call her Mary Doe. Mary had problems. The headache,
> the doctor said, came from a thickening of the skull bone
> causing pressure on the brain. A bad back operated on for
> a ruptured disc in 1963 was then reinjured. There were
> personal problems having to do with grown children. Last
> summer she had a nervous breakdown. Now she was get-
> ting help from the mental health guidance clinic, but it
> did not soothe the physical pains that often made her vir-
> tually blind.
> "A few weeks ago I was at the end of my rope," she
> said. "I felt there was no place left to turn for help. I
> really hit the bottom."
> That day a friend of hers came to her with an ad she
> found in the personal columns of this newspaper. It was an
> invitation to "sick, despondent, depressed people" to phone
> the First New Testament Prayer Tower.
> "The voice on the phone was so reassuring, so gentle,"
> Mary recalled gratefully. "The lady said prayers for
> me and quoted from the Scripture. Such comforting
> things." . . .
> The Prayer Tower consultation had such a good effect
> on Mary that she asked if she might call back the next
> day. Soon the conversations became a regular and precious
> part of Mary's day.
> "And just think. I found out the Prayer Tower lady was

a young woman with two small kids but she took time to talk to me."

When Mary decided she wanted to attend a service at the First New Testament Church arrangements were made to pick her up and bring her back home. This too became a regular part of her life. . . . Today Mary says her headaches have disappeared.

"You know, they pray over you with the laying on of hands. One day I realized I wasn't having a headache! I could hardly believe it. . . . My doctor is so pleased. He said that physicians can only go so far. They can't do everything. A lot of healing is up to God." *

Where medicine has failed, the resource made available through ordinary, loving, listening and praying people can frequently heal and change the sick and troubled. This is the priesthoood of believers in operation. I believe we need to recover this idea in more of our churches today.

In 1942 Karl Menninger said, "Love is the medicine for the sickness of the world." The kind of love Dr. Menninger was speaking of is not learned in a professional school. Love is something that all of us can receive and all of us can give. Love is being your brother's brother and helping him find his own resources, his own dignity, his strength, and his nondependence.

This is the day of the paraprofessional—the day of the layman priest. God has called his church to be a royal priesthood. This means that every believer is a priest, one who mediates strength and grace and healing from God to people. This is the exciting adventure. Each of us can be a resource to another person in the time when he is ready to grow. We can learn how to listen to people deeply, to respect them, to understand them, to empathize, to identify, to be a friend to a friend.

Fort Myers News Press article by Kathleen Powell, March 15, 1975.

Dr. Thomas Szasz, noted author and teaching psychiatrist at the Upstate Medical Center in New York, talks about unlocking the doors of the mental hospitals. He suggests that we no longer need medically trained technicians to be the guardians, keepers, and overseers of these places. He proposes, instead, running adult "orphanages" for those who cannot make it with their families or in society at the present time. They need a place where warm-hearted individuals can give custodial care, even as the Salvation Army provides food and lodging for those with physical or social needs. A great many of us without specialized training could be staff members in places like that.

The Mystique of the Nonprofessional

All of us know a great deal more than we think we do. And with each passing day and its life experiences, our training takes on new dimensions. Just because I don't have a diploma on the wall which is symbolic of years of professional training does not mean that I have no credentials to work effectively in a given field.

On the island where I live we have one of the finest small newspapers in the country. It has won many awards. The paper was started by people who had no previous experience in running papers and no journalistic training. The implications are intriguing. Actually, most of us have been reading newspapers and magazines all our lives and intuitively know good journalism from bad. Perhaps many of us without journalistic training or experience could put together a good newspaper because we are lifelong readers of newspapers. Quite likely it would only be necessary to hire journalistic expertise for the actual typesetting of articles and for layout.

A lack of credentials need not hinder us in any field.

Recently an old friend, Charles Williams, wrote me about a man from Rhodesia who ventured outside his area of expertise to tackle the problem of hunger in Africa. A fortune hunter, farmer, bush pilot, and mercenary soldier, Eric "Farlie" Winson is setting out to transform one hundred thousand acres of arid desert into lush, four-crops-a-year land. Winson was introduced to the Nigerian agricultural officer and asked to look over a plan by a German agri-engineering firm for growing peanuts in the Niger River bottom land. He was being considered for director of the project. Here's what happened next according to my friend's letter: "Following a two-week survey, he wrote such a convincing counterplan at one-third the proposed project cost that he was immediately authorized to head the project and do it his way. The original plan called for completion of the project in one year. In just two months, Farlie built five miles of canals, ten miles of roads, cleared and cultivated the land, installed the irrigation system, and in addition built his own home and equipment shops out of native materials. Mr. Winson, challenged by the opportunity to build on this base of productivity, claims that thousands of acres of fertile river land can be cultivated and irrigated for extremely modest sums of money. The conventional approaches to the problem consistently and tiresomely called for studies and more studies —of causes, consequences, and possible courses of action. But while others regret, research and restate the problem, one man is doing something now. In a reenactment of the great American epic, Farlie Winson surveyed the challenge and the rare opportunity and responded creatively." To me Farlie has become a living parable, an exemplar or model for what can happen in many areas. Tomorrow looks brighter as we realize that God is raising up all sorts of unlikely "untrained" resources for the vast and varying fields of human needs.

The Mystery of Healing

As amateurs we are more than ever aware of the need to cooperate with some force outside ourselves and outside the counselee, trainee, or patient. For when all is said and done, to be human is a mystery. Healing is a mystery. Growth is a mystery. No one learns to heal another.

The best doctors, psychiatrists, and therapists are those who know there is another force which actually does the healing. Burrswood Hospital, a center of medical and spiritual healing south of London, England, grew out of a healing experience of its founder, Dorothy Kerrin. She had been ailing for years and her death was considered imminent. She was suffering from tubercular meningitis, peritonitis, diabetes, and other complications. Too weak to lift her hands, she was fed by injections. Believing death was near, she asked for Holy Communion. When she received it, she heard a mystical voice calling her by name and proclaiming her sufferings were over; she was to get up and walk. Although she had not walked for five years, she got up and walked steadily, to the alarm and astonishment of those gathered around her deathbed. She went into the kitchen and began to eat. Overnight she was restored from an emaciated condition to one of normal health. Raised from the brink of death by mysterious forces no man could mediate, her lifework culminated in the establishment of the healing home at Burrswood.

There is an old maxim I've heard many doctors repeat reverently, "I only change the bandages; God heals the wound." This is just as true with mental and emotional healing. In all of human growth there is a third force which can be relied upon to break through and do the unexpected because we expect Him to. As amateurs, we need to be aware of this Force and to strive to work with it. If I really am not sure what to do, then I must rely even more on this Third Force for ultimate healing.

The Mystery of the Everyday

If we are to be resources for other people, it's crucial to realize that most of our contacts are not in "professional" situations. We meet people at supermarkets, in laboratories, in schools, on the job, at parties, at meetings, at conferences. Those who seek professional help are the same people we meet every day in ordinary ways and places. Beyond helping doctors with their overwhelming counseling load as a nonprofessional or helping the clergy counsel others as a layman, we need to develop an awareness that in everyday situations we have the power to bless and to heal those with whom we come into contact. Each of us has the potential to be the significant person to another in some of life's most mundane and ordinary relationships.

In high school my life swerved immeasurably and with great suddenness because of the shapeless and plain woman teacher I mentioned earlier. She's one of the most beautiful people ever to come into my life. She took time with me, saw things that no one else saw, and introduced me to friends and viewpoints that have left their stamp on me forever. During my teens, my pastor was another liberating person. One luncheon that he instigated just before I enlisted in the army during World War II did more to change the direction of my life and my awareness of God than did all of my Sunday school and church experiences up to that time. During lunch he asked what I was going to do with my life when and if I returned from the service—and whether I had considered the Christian ministry. He loved the church, he cared about me, and he suggested the idea that he thought I had the stuff and possibly the call of

Christ to serve as a clergyman. The effects of that hour-and-a-half lunch in a restaurant on Michigan Avenue in Chicago in 1943 are still with me.

God keeps challenging and liberating me through a succession of unlikely people who just happen into my life at the right time. I remember gratefully a Baptist infantry chaplain in France and Germany, a roommate in college, an elderly magazine editor in New York, and a doctor in Toronto. A parade of incongruous people have seemed to sense my particular needs at appointed times and have been God's special priests to me. It has been my highest hope for years now to be the right person at the right time in God's purpose for others. This surely is what being a resource in the relational revolution is all about in its broadest and most exciting sense—amateurs helping amateurs to become all that God meant them to be in the ordinary situations of life.

There is a wonderful story about a small boy who went to a country fair many years ago. There he saw a man selling wild birds from a cage.

"Mister," he said, "what are you going to do with the birds you don't sell when the fair is over today?"

"Kill them, I guess! What good are they?"

"Could I buy them from you? I'll give you everything I've got."

"Let me see how much it is," said the wild-bird catcher suspiciously.

The boy ran home and took all of the earnings of his short lifetime and brought them to the wild-bird catcher. It was enough! That night the boy took the birds home. His heart was full of joy and excitement and he couldn't wait to release his wild birds. But to his amazement, when he opened the door of the cage only a few of the birds chose to leave. The rest had apparently grown accustomed to their life in prison. In desperation the boy began to rattle the cage and shake it until every single bird was flying free and had once again regained his true home in the wide sky.

We need to remind one another that at a great price God has opened the cage door for everyone. As resource people in the relational revolution we can become fellow cage-rattlers who will settle for nothing less for each other than freedom, flight, and wide horizons.

Footnote to Chapter 7

In reading this chapter for the last time, I am aware that I need to clarify two basic points. First of all, it is not my intention in any way to downgrade the professionals in any field. There are never enough well-trained and highly motivated professionals. Rather, my purpose in writing this chapter is to attempt to upgrade and encourage the amateurs—to raise our expectations for one another in fields in which we have had no formal training.

Further, I in no way meant to imply that the average man in the street without any training can function as a counselor as well as most professionals. Actually, in all the tests referred to in this chapter comparing the "results" for those helped by professionals as over against those helped by un-trained persons, the untrained were given "permission" or "status" in some way by the very professionals who recruited them. Obviously these are situations where first of all the self-concept of the amateur counselor was altered. Secondly, the expectation of the counselee was raised by the fact that the "counselor" was assumed to be a professional. The tests certainly indicate that amateurs given the right setting and "permission" can be most effective. But that does not mean that those conditions automatically prevail when-ever two untrained people meet in a social setting.

8. WHAT ABOUT TOMORROW?

MARK TWAIN once defined spring fever in this way: "You don't know quite what it is you do want, but it just fairly makes your heart ache you want it so." Hope, one of the most valuable and dynamic gifts God can give us, is perhaps not unlike spring fever in that it is often difficult to describe just what it is you hope for.

I think I mentioned earlier my belief that we are possibly in a pre- rather than a post-Christian era. My convictions are probably closely tied to my hope—hope in something I cannot prove conclusively and find difficult even to describe. But let's assume for now that we are in a pre-Christian era and raise the question, "What about tomorrow?" If we are in some kind of a spiritual renaissance, how will tomorrow be different from today? Historians have told us that ten years before the Renaissance, when the Western world was so totally in the grip of the Dark Ages, even the wisest person alive had no clue that a change was coming. The new era broke with the sudden drama of a sunrise at sea.

If ancient wise men could not perceive the coming of that Renaissance, how can I presume to suggest what our tomorrow might be like? I can only attribute my presumption to a yearning in me something like Mark Twain's spring fever.

But that ache is not entirely subjective. The Bible has a great deal to say about the implications and effects of the Messiah's coming. Perhaps the best known of these prophecies comes from Isaiah 40:3-5: "The voice of him that crieth in the wilderness, prepare ye the way of the Lord, make straight in the desert a highway for our God. Every valley shall be exalted, and every mountain and hill shall be made low: and the crooked shall be made straight, and the rough places plain: and the glory of the Lord shall be revealed, and all flesh shall see it together: for the mouth of the Lord has spoken it" (KJV).

This description surely gives us a clue about the Christian era. Mankind will no longer be separated by the valleys and the mountains. All of life will be a whole. God meant us to be one people. Divisions of brother from brother or group from group are not God's ultimate plan for mankind on this tiny planet. What happens to you happens to me. What happens to me happens to you.

So my dream for tomorrow centers in a world in which the coming of Christ removes those valley or mountain barriers that keep us from a shared life—a life of intimacy, conviviality, communion, and belonging. The relational society then is a demonstration of the Messiah's coming. The Christian era will emerge when, as we've said in the last chapter, all of mankind becomes a resource for the leveling of the mountains and the filling in of the valleys which separate and divide. Healers and priests of one another, we will be co-workers in the removal of the barriers that keep us from our true destiny as one people on one planet to whom the Messiah has come.

What are some of the barriers which I hope will be erased in the new day ahead? First of all, there is the barrier of age. I begin with this one because in my loneliness, self-consciousness, and estrangement I have often cut myself off from the resources of love and fellowship of people both older and younger than I. Let us hope that the relational society will be an ageless society where we cry and laugh and hope and pray together at every age.

The revelation in this area came to me only last year. On Mother's Day, my wife and I visited my mother in the delightful retirement village where she now lives. It is a church-related community, and Mother has taken up with a marvelous group of women, all committed Christians with sound doctrinal underpinnings and a keen nose for the untrue, unethical, or heretical. But whenever one of them sends me a tract or an article or a booklet, I tend to feel they are finding me doctrinally or morally unacceptable or suspicious (my wife tells me I suffer from paranoia). My real problem is that I have always been intimidated by those who are older—especially if they have been Christians for decades longer than I. I assume they are wiser and sounder and that they suffer and succumb less to temptation than I do. Too often I interpret their sincere desire to help me as an attempt to straighten me out, and I become hostile or withdraw.

This then was the setting for last Mother's Day. We joined my mother for worship at her church, of course, although not without misgivings on my part. From either pulpit or pew, Mother's Day is probably my least favorite day in the church, for if I am preaching I never know quite what to say about mothers without sounding maudlin or dishonest, and I'm always fearful of hearing some eulogy that seems to make mothers more than human and therefore less than human. The preacher did a really good job, however, as he honored mothers and made them people along with the rest of us. But my anxiety rose when I saw a huge collection of carnations on the pulpit. "Here it comes," I thought. "After the sermon he is going to present a carnation to every mother and all the women without children are going to feel second class." But not so. Instead he invited each woman present to come and take a carnation in memory of her mother—red for a mother still living and white if she were dead. As is all too often the case, a great many more women than men have lasted until retirement and of the five hundred people in church, four hundred were women with an average age of about seventy-five. They began to line up, some erect women looking younger than their years, some bent or stooped, others with canes, crutches, walkers, and wheelchairs. Most had white hair or blue hair, and some had almost no hair.

One by one this glorious company filed by the altar and received their carnations, and almost all were white ones. Clutching their special flower, they went back to their pews, wiping tears from their eyes. I suddenly realized that there are no old ladies; there are just little girls, many of whom grow up and have babies and become mommies to other little girls. To think of others being old and therefore different is to miss the wonder that we are all born children, die children, and ultimately inhabit that mystical kingdom of our Lord only as little children. This glimpse into life as a whole with no age differences has begun to change my relationship to older people. They are simply people very much like me; some better, some worse, but not different.

Somehow I seem to have allowed myself to be intimidated by the young as well. Even when I was young myself I was not at home among them. It was as if I'd been born old and awkward, without the carefree attitude I so often envy in my own three children and their friends. As the years have gone by I have admired more and more that freedom I felt I never had and certainly do not now have. But I am reaping one benefit—it's great to be a parent at a time when your children feel so free about clothes that you can send them off to college with only a brown bag full of patched and faded blue jeans. Still, I am discovering that young people today are not as free in this area as I had assumed. They may wear ragged, patched clothes, but the rags are very carefully chosen and the patches are works of art. The fact that young people are probably as hung-up about dress as I was and am has helped me fear them less and love them more.

In the same way it is my hope that the young can stop putting the middle-aged group in a box. Though the myth of the generation gap is a myth that has made strangers of the generations, in our dreams and aspirations we are not so different. I love the story of the teenager who announced to his parents, "Listen. I'm leaving home. There is nothing you can do to stop me. I want excitement, adventure, money, and beautiful women. I'll never find them here, so I'm leaving. Just don't try to stop me." As he headed for the door, his father leaped up and ran toward him. "Dad," said the boy, "you heard what I said. Don't try to stop me." "Who's trying to stop you?" retorted his father. "I'm going with you." When life is a whole no chronological mountains or valleys separate people. Some of us have lived longer and have had more experiences but we are all children living in an ageless society.

Another barrier which separates us comes from our attempt to compartmentalize our lives. We play a role in public that has little to do with what we really are and what we feel and think in our innermost being. Recently my wife and I were sightseeing in a marvelous fortress in Salzburg, Austria. The tour from room to room took us to the torture chamber where as recently as the late nineteenth century the resident ruler was still torturing victims in grotesque ways with racks, ovens, screws, and iron maidens. Leaving there, we went up several flights of stairs to the royal chambers. Almost directly above the torture chamber we saw the ruler's private chapel. We were told he never missed his morning and evening meditations. It seemed incredible to us that the private prayers of one devout ruler were being punctuated by the screams of his enemies being tortured in the same building.

But perhaps this is not so different from what happens today. We may jealously guard our private morality yet do the expedient thing in our public life because "it's a jungle out there" or because "that's the way life is." While our government was going through the infamous and shattering Watergate experience, the Boy Scouts of America had their own Watergate. Their chief executive announced publicly that many Scout executives had been cheating. In order to receive additional funds for their program they padded their membership figures. Over a four-year period, a Chicago Boy Scout council received $341,000 in federal funds to work with forty thousand poor youngsters. I suppose their motives were good; they could do a better job with more money. But the point is that men who in private life might meticulously correct an error against them at the supermarket can lie unflinchingly when hundreds of thousands of dollars of federal funds are involved. No one can live two lives, being one person in public and another person in private. The collusion that goes on in society which allows this causes a national schizophrenia and a great deal of harm to us as individuals.

In an issue on "Watergating On Main Street," *Saturday Review* examined ethical standards in seven professions. Max Lerner introduced the whole discussion. What went wrong? "In many cases—law, medicine, business, politics, journalism, accounting—the social structures that held the

professions in balance internally have broken down. . . .
Imperative for the professions is a sense of wholeness. The
worst thing that has happened to professionals has been
the divorce between their professional and business life and
their personal life. It is a fateful dualism, this effort to
separate the kind of person I am in my profession from
the kind of person I am with my children, friends, wife,
husband, lover. . . . We have no effective way of compart-
mentalizing ourselves without confusing our sense of moral
direction."

Lerner adds, "I like to get paid for my work, but what
fulfills me and makes me whole is the work, not the payment. I am involved with both, but if I am to be a whole
person, I must know what is primary for me and what is
secondary. If I know that the quality and integrity of my
work come first, then I am true to my profession both as
writer and as teacher. If the money comes first, then I am
corrupt—even if I never steal anything or accept a bribe.
If I am unsure about which comes first, then I am morally
confused and a divided person."

If life is a whole, then the barriers between a public and
a private life need to be erased. For the lawyer, doctor,
teacher, businessman, clergyman or whatever, why should
there be a separation of life into public and private catego-
ries, any more than there should be a division into secular
and sacred? Life is a whole, and the relational society will
come as our dualistic approach to life is overcome.

If, then, in the relational society our public and private
lives must be made one, so too must we overcome the dis-
parity between our words and our actions. What we are and
what we say must be integrated. I suppose there is nothing
new about being in love with words for their own sake, but
from Christian leaders, from intellectual eggheads, from the
media at every level come so many of them we must surely

be described as a nation of wordaholics. I, for one, am
tired of them. Sadder yet, I am tired to my own. Unless
there is a correlation between words and substance, words
and actions, words and reality, words are hollow, empty
things.

Take world hunger, for just one example. This is an area
in which it is imperative that we end the gulf between our
words and our actions. Most Americans feel compassion and
even guilt about the great bulk of people all over the world
who are perpetually hungry or even starving to death. To
help, we take up offerings in our churches, we adopt overseas orphans or send regular CARE packages. National leaders call for days of fasting to raise funds for overseas
relief. In spite of all this, it is a fact that America operates
in the world grain market much as the Arabs operate in the
world oil market. Ninety-five percent of our grain reserves
are controlled by six giant American-based multinational
agribusinesses. These six agribusinesses state openly that
their goal is not to feed hungry people, but to make profits
for their stockholders. Their business is to sell food, and
most of the hungry in the world are too poor to buy food.

Recently in India's West Bengal one thousand people
starved to death within sight of food they could not afford to
buy. That one incident provides a parable for the whole
world. There is actually sufficient food but there is no motivation for releasing it to those who cannot afford to buy it.
Recent surveys prove that food production is growing faster
than the population. Hunger is the result of distribution,
not production. Third and fourth and fifth world nations
produce entire crops for our benefit. There are countries
which export their entire peanut crop, for example, while
the poor do not have the funds to import grains from Europe
and America.

But it is not just in the areas of food distribution or international politics that our words and actions are so disparate. A friend of mine in New York worked for one of the large advertising companies. He was assigned to create a commercial for a local beer company. This gifted friend came up with what was at that time one of the first really humorous commercials. He created two cartoon-character brothers who supposedly owned this brewery and two of the funniest radio comics around were hired as their voices. The commercials were a huge success and beer sales skyrocketed. But when after a few years sales began to drop off, the brewery switched their advertising to another firm. Later surveys proved that because of the popular commercial, people in unprecedented numbers had rushed out to buy the beer, only to find that it was terrible beer. Rather than improve the quality of the beer, the brewery changed their advertising.

To me, this seems to be a real parallel to the church and its evangelism program. The words we preach about God's love and the fellowship of his people seem unrelated to what is experienced in the local church. There is a great gulf between what is promised by mass evangelists, radio or TV evangelists, mail evangelists or door-to-door evangelists and what worshipers find the expression of God's love to be in most local churches. When the church can help people to discover that God is real, that his people will accept them as they are, that they will be included and affirmed and encouraged to find themselves and their gifts, the word will spread. The reality of the experience will almost vitiate the need for evangelism on a large scale. If we in the church cannot deliver what we have promised, all of the words cannot prevent seekers from becoming disillusioned and dropping away.

I hope our relational society will also bridge the gulf between such traditionally alienated groups as labor and management. I look for a time when labor and management will discover their mutual dependency and encourage each other toward making life better for all of us. Unfortunately, the gulf between labor and management, or capital and labor, is still enormous in most parts of the world, and not without cause. Years ago capital made serfs of people and robber barons were little better than slaveholders. But the revolution that was needed has come, and now labor seems to hold the gun to the head of management. We are all suffering from the resulting impasse.

Recently relatives from Sweden visited us. Having never been to my ancestral home, I was appalled to learn from my cousin what happened sixty years ago when my grandfather, a substantial businessman, died in middle age. The courts decided he had more liabilities than assets and so stripped his widow of everything she owned. With eleven children she was literally put into the streets, while all her belongings, including her wedding ring, were sold. She was permitted by law to keep just one bed for every two children. Ultimately, she was able to find a one-room apartment to house all those beds and children and to try to make a living as a seamstress.

Certainly, Sweden has come a long way in sixty years. Today in this most enlightened of all socialist countries the taxes are enormous but the working man has ultimate security. Still, I am personally wary of such an extreme kind of socialism, not because of my politics but because of my theology. I am enough of a Calvinist to be concerned about what happens to citizens of a state where no one is allowed to fail.

Recently I was interviewing one of Germany's leading psychiatrists. He operates a clinic for alcoholics and neurotics in the Black Forest area of Germany. I asked him how the clinic was supported financially. Explaining that if the patients or the families cannot pay, the government underwrites their expenses, he went on to say this: "You know, Bruce, today in Germany no one is allowed to fail. A hundred years ago families sent their black sheep to America. People arriving in America at that time in history either had to make good or die. Your country was made great by those same black sheep. They built America and in the process found their own lives. Today in both your country and mine, few are allowed to fail and therefore never have the chance to find themselves."

I'm sure this theory made a great impression on me because it is one that reinforces my own prejudices. Nevertheless it seems a reality of life that people work together for good primarily out of enlightened self-interest.

Many years ago I served a church in a small Illinois town where half the citizens were employed by a local coal mine. The hatred between the mine owners and the workers was enormous. The miners took great pleasure in sabotaging production in the mine. By breaking machines, delaying and generally goofing off, they raised the cost per ton of coal and thereby "got at" their employers. It was their way of expressing their anger, justifiable or not. One Friday night with no warning all the employees received pink slips indicating that they were fired on the spot. This spelled economic catastrophe to individuals and to the town as a whole. The community has not fully recovered yet, for the mine never reopened.

I'm suggesting that whenever enmity exists between two groups working together the consequences are tragic for both. In this instance, had churches been concerned about reconciliation between miners and company, much suffering and financial loss could have been eliminated. Because we were not faithful in trying to reconcile neighbors to their employers, neighbors suffered and the town suffered. Know-

ing God's mandates to level the mountains and fill in the
valleys that separate warring groups has enormous consequences.

At least one place where reconciliation is taking place between labor and management is at the Rushton Mining
Company in Pennsylvania. Consultant Eric Trist of the University of Pennsylvania has helped form a steering committee composed of management and members of the United
Mine Workers. The committee set up experimental work
groups of nine men—one team on each shift made up of
volunteers from the regular work force. Each of the men
was trained to do all of the jobs so that he could fill any
vacancy on the team. And all of the men earn top pay.
Safety was the shift foreman's job, but the production of
coal and working grievances were the crew's responsibility.

This experiment has paid off in a number of ways. The
mine is saving money even though group payrolls are higher.
The groups boast lower supply costs, higher production
rates, less absenteeism, less turnover, and the lowest number of safety violations in the mine's history. The biggest
payoff is in the workers' cooperative spirit. As one man
expressed it: "Suddenly we felt that we mattered to somebody. Somebody trusted us—when a machine busts down
nowadays, most of the time we don't bother to call a main-
tenance man. We fix it ourselves, because, like I said, we
feel it is as much ours as our car at home."

The men often remain in the locker room after hours to
settle problems and discuss the next day's work. The re-
searchers say it is too early to draw conclusions from this
experiment, but I am encouraged by it. It is one place where
barriers are being removed between two mutually dependent groups to the benefit of both and to all of society.

What about tomorrow in terms of the church? My own

dream is that, in the relational society to come, the mountains and the valleys that separate religion from reality will be removed. The architecture of our churches, the kind of music we hear and the language of the services, the hour or day of the week of the service, the fact that we sit on the floor on cushions or in straight-backed pews is almost totally unimportant. The essential fact is that the grace of God be proclaimed in terms that affect the lives of the worshipers.

Often religion becomes an esoteric eddy. Like an art form that attracts admirers, a sermon or a worship service can be "enjoyed" by churchgoers or they can find it long and dull. This is quite apart from whether or not it has had anything to say about their lives and involvements at that point in time. The pastor of our church has a brother-in-law who lives in the Middle East and frequently broadcasts in Arabic. He has an enormous following because he has immersed himself in Arab culture. The Arabs say of him, "He knows the heart of the Arab village." Would that more preachers knew the heart of their congregation and could proclaim a gospel in terms of issues central to them.

Once at a luncheon I remember asking one pastor what the concerns of his congregation were. He didn't seem to understand me. "Well," I explained, "what topic could you announce for your sermon next Sunday that would insure getting 90 percent of your people out to church?" "I don't know," he confessed after a long pause. I really don't mean to suggest that every sermon be Number One in the interest polls, but it does seem to me that an effective pastor ought to know some of the topics central to the lives of his congregation if he is relevantly to proclaim at that time and in that place the Gospel of Jesus Christ. I am hopeful that in the relational society of tomorrow, religion and the reality of life's issues will be one—just as they were from the time of the Old Testament prophets and on through the New Testament.

Another barrier I should like to see disappear in the relational society of tomorrow is the one which separates those who nourish and emphasize the inner life from those whose life-style is marked by social involvement and action. This division is not only found in the Christian camp. In a strictly secular sense and unrelated to any religion, transcendental meditation, for example, is sweeping the country. Self-understanding and self-fulfillment are in a large sense the goals of such diverse methods as gestalt, Arica, Earhart Seminar Training, and others. But those who practice only introspection, either secular or sacred, are in danger of engaging in what has been called the new narcissism. In the Christian tradition we have a double emphasis, a combination of being still and listening for the still small voice and also of giving a cup of cold water in Jesus' name. I am encouraged personally by the new emphasis on meditation, mysticism, and the inward look. I see it as part of the answer, provided it does not become an end in itself. The authentic Christian life-style, I am convinced, is one of prayer and authentic mysticism which results in responsible involvement with the world and its problems.

Listen to what G. K. Chesterton wrote about the distinctive mark of Christianity in his *Orthodoxy*: "No two ideals could be more opposite than a Christian saint in a Gothic cathedral and a Buddhist saint in a Chinese temple. The opposition exists at every point; but perhaps the shortest statement of it is that the Buddhist saint always has his eyes shut, while the Christian saint always has them very wide open. The Buddhist saint has a sleek and harmonious body, but his eyes are heavy and sealed with sleep. The medieval saint's body is wasted to its crazy bones, but his eyes are frightfully alive. . . . Granted that both images are extravagances. . . . It must be a real divergence which could produce such opposite extravagants. The Buddhist is looking with a peculiar intentness inwards. The Christian is staring with a frantic intentness outwards." * Perhaps as Eastern and Western culture become even more integrated, we can utilize both the inward and the outward look since both are necessary to authentic living.

Finally it is my hope that in the relational society of tomorrow life will be not a puzzle to be figured out nor a game to be won but a celebration. Furthermore, I'm certain that this is most of all what God intended for us. This truth came to me with beautiful suddenness recently. Hazel and I were in Europe for three weeks partly on business. While there, we received two letters on the very same day. They were from two of our children who have grown and left home. One is in law school and the other is starting his journalistic career on a newspaper. With no apparent collusion, these two letters seemed to have the same kind of message. Neither had any unusual successes to report (i.e., social, vocational, academic, or financial)! But both letter writers seemed filled with joy and celebration in being who they were and where they were at the time they were writing. Their letters were satisfying to receive, but beyond that, they made me aware of what God the Father must hope for in all of us as his children—that we find the joy of being the people he created, delighting in where we are and what we are doing. It is my dream that in the relational society of tomorrow we will find a new way to relate to one another as persons filled with a sense of wonder and celebration for who we are, where we are, and the opportunities

*Fontana Books, 1961, pp. 130–31.

that are before us in service and in meaningful relationships. Perhaps all the world will be able to celebrate the fact that we belong to one another and are part of one global family.

Earlier on that same trip, we had the fun of being in Munich at the time of *Oktoberfest*. We were excited to be there at that special time when the Germans pitch great tents and for several weeks celebrate their Germanness with singing and dancing, drinking and eating. The first night we walked into a huge tent full of thousands of people. An enormous German band was playing. We wanted so much to share in the food and the fun, yet every table was filled. We did not speak the language. We did not know how to engage a waitress or get service or find a seat. We wandered through that tent like two little orphans wanting so much to join the celebration and not knowing how.

We were about to give up and go back to our hotel, tired of being only spectators at this amazingly unique national celebration, when suddenly across a dozen or more tables a man stood up and waved in our direction. I was certain he did not mean me, but I looked around and could see no one standing anywhere near me. Smiling and nodding, the man pointed to me and beckoned again. "Me?" I called in English. The man nodded. With that we went over to his table. All the people there were Germans; none of them spoke English. But they had two free seats and they motioned for us to sit down. We were no longer strangers. We belonged. We were being included in the celebration.

All of us, in our hometown or in some foreign country, in our own church or someone else's church or no church, long to be those who are included in whatever is going on. I want someone to stand up and point to me and beckon me to come over and join in. When it happens, though, we are all as surprised as I was at *Oktoberfest*. Somehow we grow up expecting to be rejected. We're not even surprised when we're not included. We begin early to guard against feeling like outsiders with our noses pressed to the window of someone else's party.

The New Yorker magazine of September 1975 carried an account of a nursery school excursion. Six boys named Kevin were on the bus, and somehow one of them had been left behind in the park where the children had been playing for about an hour. Frantically, those in charge returned to the park and found the little lost Kevin in the hands of a kindly man who had bought him an ice cream cone. Oddly enough, it was discovered later that every single child on that bus had known that one of the Kevins was missing, but they had not mentioned it to the driver or the teacher or even to each other. They just took it for granted that Kevin had been left forever for some reason they did not know.

Like those children, most of us have been conditioned to accept the fact that at some time we too will be left behind and we are resigned to it. Some fate decrees these things and we can't fight it. In the relational society of tomorrow, let's expect the reverse. When one of us is left out, missing, or lost, the rest of us will set up a hue and cry and demand, "Where is the lost one? We must find him. We cannot live our lives without the whole group."